Out Out Out Out Out Out Out Out Out Out Out Out Out

No Ball No Ball No Ball No Ball No Ball No Ball No Ball No Ball No

Not Out Not Out Not Out Not Out Not Out Not

Wide Wide Wide Wide Wide Wide Wide Wide Wide Wide Wide Wide

Leg-bye Leg-bye Leg-bye Leg-bye Leg-bye Leg-bye Leg-bye Leg-bye Leg-bye

Six Six Six Six Six Six Six Six Six Six Six Six Six Six Six Six Six Six Si

Out Out Out Out Out Out Out Out Out Out Out Out Out Out

Four Four Four Four Four Four Four Four Four Four Four Four Four Four

Not Out Not Out Not Out Not Out Not Out Not Out Not Out Not

Wide Wide Wide Wide Wide Wide Wide Wide Wide Wide Wide Wide Wid

No Ball No Ball No Ball No Ball No Ball No Ball No Ball No Ball No

Out Out Out Out Out Out Out Out Out Out Out Out Out Out

Six Six Six Six Six Six Six Six Six Six Six Six Six Six Six Six Six

Leg-bye Leg-bye Leg-bye Leg-bye Leg-bye Leg-bye Leg-bye Leg-bye Leg-bye

Four Four Four Four Four Four Four Four Four Four Four Four Four Four

Out Out Out Out Out Out Out Out Out Out Out Out Out Out

No Ball No Ball No Ball No Ball No Ball No Ball No Ball No Ball No

Not Out Not Out Not Out Not Out Not Out Not Out Not Out Not

Wide Wide Wide Wide Wide Wide Wide Wide Wide Wide

D0997087

From Claire and Christine Christmas 1999

That's Out!

DICKIE BIRD

That's Out!
DICKIE BIRD

WEIDENFELD & NICOLSON
LONDON

Half-title page: Harold Dennis 'Dickie' Bird.
Title page: Umpire Dickie Bird on the balcony of the Lord's pavilion in 1996
following his final Test match.

First published in the United Kingdom in 1985 by Arthur Barker Limited,
a subsidiary of Weidenfeld (Publishers) Ltd
This edition published in 1999 by Weidenfeld & Nicolson
Text copyright © Dickie Bird & John Callaghan, 1985, 1999
Design and layout copyright © Weidenfeld & Nicolson, 1999
Picture selections and captions by Weidenfeld & Nicolson, 1999

All rights reserved. No part of this publication may be reproduced
in any material form (including photocopying or storing it
in any medium by electronic means and whether or not transiently or
incidentally to some other use of this publication) without the written
permission of the copyright owner, except in accordance with the
provisions of the Copyright, Designs and Patents Act 1988 or under
the terms of a licence issued by the Copyright Licensing Agency,
90 Tottenham Court Road, London W1P 9HE. Applications for the
copyright owner's written permission to reproduce any part of this
publication should be addressed to the publisher.

The picture acknowledgements on p. 159 constitute an extension
to this copyright page
A CIP catalogue record for this book is available from the British Library
ISBN 0 297 82527 5

Designed by Harry Green
Typeset in Minion
Printed in Great Britain by Butler and Tanner

Weidenfeld & Nicolson
Illustrated Division
The Orion Publishing Group
Wellington House
125 Strand
London
WC2R 0BB

Contents

Acknowledgements

THIS BOOK could not have been written, nor, indeed, could I have enjoyed my life in cricket, without the help and encouragement of many people. I would especially like to thank John Callaghan, with whom I collaborated closely throughout on the production; also Patrick Eagar, Ken Kelly, Clem Newham and Keith Lodge, the sports editor of the *Barnsley Chronicle* and his staff; Roy Ullyett, cartoonist for the *Daily Express*; photographers Geoff Richards, Stan Bulmer, Don Oakes, Roy Sabine, the firm of Stan Plus and Stan Two; Benny Hill, sports editor of the *Sheffield Morning Telegraph* and his staff, the sports editor and staff of the *Daily Mirror*, the *Coal News*, the *Sheffield Star*, the *Yorkshire Post* and *Yorkshire Evening Post*; the staff of Yorkshire Television and BBC North; Gubby Allen (cricket administrator) for all his help and kindness; and particularly Donald Carr, the secretary of the Test and County Cricket Board.

Foreword by Dennis Lillee
(Western Australia and Australia)

Big wicket – Dennis Lillee and Graham Yallop celebrate after combining to dismiss Geoff Boycott for 137, England v. Australia, The Oval, 1981.

Harold dennis 'dickie' bird! The name was enough to intrigue me when we first met as umpire and player but it certainly did not indicate the nature of this great official and great man.

Dickie is the ideal umpire, one who played the game at county level and has a genuine understanding of the people he is controlling during each game. He knows when to talk to the players, when to joke with them and when and how to discipline them, but, above all, his ability to make correct decisions is, in my opinion, second to none.

Then there is the other side of the person and that is the man. His dry humour has always amused me and I will quote one example of this.

At the Oval during the 1975 Australian tour of England I requested a change of a rather battered ball which was out of shape. Dickie looked at it, handed it back and told me to complete the over. I wasn't happy with this as the ball was definitely not up to the expected standards for a Test. I could not hope to work miracles with it, so I threw it across to my captain, Ian Chappell. He said: 'I realize it is out of shape, but complete the over with it and I'll have a chat to Dickie.' That didn't suit me, either, so I protested by delivering two good length, well flighted off-spinners, telling Dickie in no uncertain terms that the ball could be used only by the slower men.

His serious reaction and dead straight face merely masked his thoughts, for when Ian came up at the end of the over to bargain for a better ball, Dickie said: 'I wouldn't change either the ball or the bowler. He's the best off-spinner I've seen all season.' Being the fair and reasonable man he is, though, he immediately met our request.

There are many more stories about Dickie in this book and I hope you enjoy them as much as I did. To Harold Dennis 'Dickie' Bird, a friend and a very fine umpire, all the best and many thanks for all those hours out in the middle.

Dennis Lillee

Introduction

I WOULD HAVE LOVED to have been an England cricketer. Like thousands of other boys born into the traditional stronghold of the game, the Broad Acres, I nursed the thought of being good enough to represent both my county and country through hours of practice, and this goal, distant though it may have been, helped me to overcome the disappointments that are part and parcel of every sporting life.

There was, for example, a disastrous first visit to the Yorkshire nets when, against some hostile bowling from the likes of Fred Trueman, Bob Appleyard and Johnny Wardle, I seemed to get everything wrong and kept having to put up my stumps after ball upon ball had sent them flying. Lashed by the rough edge of senior coach Arthur Mitchell's tongue, I felt very much out of my depth.

'Ticker', as everybody called him, did, however, see some talent as I batted on, and I like to think that I achieved a fairly good standard in my time with Yorkshire between 1956 and 1959. Those were the years when my hopes of making the grade as a batsman were still very real, but I did not have much success after moving down to Leicestershire and I never settled in at Grace Road.

I was pretty miserable as my career came to an end, but now I am able to look back with the benefit of hindsight and say that the failure to establish myself was the finest thing that happened. Just a few more runs and the painful decision that I had to leave Leicestershire to concentrate on coaching might not have been made as I continued to pitch my skills against the bowlers on the county circuit, although in my heart of hearts I have to accept that I would never have taken part in a Test match as a player.

The fact that I have had the privilege of being associated with so many Tests as an umpire underlines the point that fate did me a kindness. I reckon that barring illness or injury I can stay on the umpires' list until I am sixty-five – a span which covers two normal playing lifetimes.

Often in sport when you feel on top of the world something comes along to bring you smartly back down to earth. I remember all too well putting together

my highest score in first-class cricket – 181 not out off the Glamorgan attack at Park Avenue, Bradford, in 1959 – and thinking as I walked off the field that I had really broken through. Not a bit of it! Next day I reported back with the Colts. But there was no point in grumbling or getting a chip on my shoulder. I got on with the job, consoling myself with the thought that I still had a place in a squad of fine Yorkshire players.

On the other hand, on occasions when you are down, an important bit of good luck is waiting just around the corner. It was a wrench when I left Leicestershire and turned my attentions to club cricket as player and coach. I experienced no sense of bitterness and the people in Devon, where I worked with Paignton and Plymouth College, showed me a lot of kindness, but reading every day about the happenings on the county circuit and noting the scores stimulated a natural desire to retrace my steps in some way.

I had never seriously considered umpiring, but when the opportunity arose to join the first-class list I jumped at it and I have never for a single second regretted that move. Life has, in fact, been very good to me throughout the thirty-seven years that have rolled past so quickly since I graduated to the adult world as a fifteen-year-old with Barnsley in the Yorkshire League.

There has never been a time when I have not been in a job that has provided both a clean living and some marvellous friendships. In a way, too, I have become an ambassador for cricket, meeting with leading figures in so many walks of life. One particular gathering that stands out followed an invitation from the Prime Minister, Mrs Margaret Thatcher, to attend a reception at 10 Downing Street on Thursday, 21 November 1981.

That became one of the longest and coldest afternoons I have endured. We were all supposed to be there for 6.30 pm, but, of course, I turned up at 4.00 pm, walking briskly up and down Whitehall, past the Horse Guards, determined not to be late. I strolled about at the top of Downing Street, trying to keep warm as I kept checking my watch, urging the minutes to tick away.

The policeman on duty recognized me and we had a chat. 'Bit early, Dickie,' he suggested. 'Just a couple of hours or so,' I agreed. He grinned sympathetically and told me that there was a good café just a few minutes down the road, so there I sat over several cups of tea, at least sheltered from the icy blast.

I was put at my ease as soon as I finally got inside the doors of Number 10, for among the throng of well-known faces, such as Terry Wogan and Peter West, stood Joe Gormley. 'Now then, Birdie, how are thee?' he demanded in his familiar voice. There is, I am sure, nothing so comforting as the sound of your native accent when you are a bit anxious.

Ernie Wise and the late Eric Morecambe were also among the guests and Eric revealed a genuine enthusiasm for cricket as he kept me talking for a long time. Dennis Thatcher used to be a Rugby Union referee, which meant we had something in common, too, and the evening went by in a flash of fascinating conversation. Afterwards, Roy Mason, MP for Barnsley, took me on a conducted tour of the Houses of Parliament before driving me back up the motorway – a gesture which rounded off the sort of day that, but for sport, I could have only dreamed about.

The sense of belonging in cricket is very special to me, possibly because my parents taught me from an early age that you must contribute to anything worthwhile before you can expect to get something out of it and they instilled into me the idea that respect has to be earned. I have, therefore, never wavered in my loyalty to the Test and County Cricket Board, who employ me. Offers from unofficial organisations never held any attraction. Approaches by representatives of Kerry Packer, who set up a kind of cricket circus in opposition to the established game, and by the men behind the rebel tour by English players to South Africa in 1981 sounded all right from a financial point of view, but there are things that money cannot buy.

My relationship with the TCCB and the players is beyond price and I am more than satisfied with my standard of living. Like anyone else I can wear only one suit at a time and I have never been one for the bright lights. I do not smoke, and I drink no more than an occasional glass of lager while relaxing with friends. Simple, straightforward home cooking is good enough for me and I see no reason to move from my eighteenth century cottage on the outskirts of Barnsley. John Wesley, the great English divine, once slept in the bedroom that I now occupy, so I am in good company at home, just as I am at 'work'.

There is, though, just one snag with the house. The previous owners kept a peacock and offered to let me keep it when I moved in. I did not regard this as practical because I am away so often, so we found the bird a home just a few hundred yards away. What I did not know is that peacocks have a habit of returning to the places with which they are most familiar. One morning I awoke to the sound of a pack of wolves having a rare old time in my garden. That, certainly, was what it sounded like. In reality, the peacock had returned and brought a mate with it, so I had a noisy disturbance until I got the pair moved back up the road.

After a hard time at a match I don't want to be roused at 5.30 every morning, so I am hoping that I shall persuade the peacocks to settle in their new surroundings.

I have a strong faith and, whenever possible, go to church on a Sunday. I also umpire on the Sabbath, of course, but I do not regard this as undermining my

beliefs, because religion encompasses many activities and is something you carry in your heart and mind whatever you are doing.

Shortly after Packer had burst onto the cricket scene in 1977 I paid a private visit to Australia and met Tony Greig. The former England captain and Sussex all-rounder has taken to the way of life 'down under', and he told me: 'We would have made you a very rich man if you had joined up with us.' I countered by telling him that he could not have made me a happier man, which was more important.

After all, nobody can take his money with him, although I suspect I know one who might try – my very good friend Geoff Boycott.

I have been lucky to umpire all over the world, meeting so many wonderful people along the way. It might be said that I am married to cricket. It is true that from time to time I miss having a family of my own. Fortunately my sister Marjorie is usually on hand to sort me out, while I have been blessed with superb neighbours in Helen, Mick and Matthew Hodder. Mick is a butcher and makes sure I eat pretty well.

My solicitor Duncan Mutch, who completed a remarkable double by becoming a vice-president of Lancashire while serving as Yorkshire's legal adviser, is a good friend, as is his wife, Kath, and I ought to record that in his day he produced a mean left-arm spinner.

I am also grateful for the generous hospitality of John and Pat Perry, who own a couple of hotels in Torquay, Livermead House and Livermead Cliff, where I often spend ten days or so at the end of a season. I need a bit of time to unwind after spending around five months keyed up. I also enjoy a spell on my own with a few records and a good book, usually, I must admit, about cricket. Diana Ross, Randy Crawford, Gladys Knight and Shirley Bassey are my favourite singers – I suppose if they had been born men they would all have been fast bowlers.

Then there is Barnsley Football Club, where I am always made so very welcome. Sometimes I bump into Boycott there and we both have a soft spot for the Oakwell lads, who never lack in honest endeavour. That just about sums up things for me – homely and honest – two little words that say so much about people, places and, I hope, me.

David Shepherd looks on as Bird receives attention
after being hit during the Old Trafford Test between
England and Australia, 1985.

1

The Man in the Middle

A FIRST-CLASS UMPIRE can suddenly feel very lonely, even though he is surrounded by players, many of whom he can count as friends, and, in the case of big matches, thousands of spectators. When the time comes to make a difficult decision, he is on his own. The responsibility cannot be shared and he has seconds in which to sort out things in his mind, well aware that he cannot win. Whatever he does, there will be those who criticize.

The long-service men who go on to reach the top become accustomed to living with pressure and I do not worry because I know that, like my colleagues, I have given an honest opinion on what I have seen.

Generally, lbw is fairly straightforward. Unless I am absolutely convinced that the ball, having been pitched on an approved line, would have hit the stumps, I turn down an appeal.

Catches close in from bat and pad or sometimes pad and bat can be tricky and so can those leg-side efforts which leave the batsman all tucked up and deviate very little as the ball passes close to the body. The umpire has to decide whether the ball actually touched anything that would rule the batsman out. He is not helped by the fact that there is a lot of appealing, no doubt influenced by the large sums of money involved in cricket these days.

I do not suggest for one minute that there is a lot of cheating. It is just that many players clutch at straws, hoping that the batsman might be out, rather like the fielders from long leg and extra cover who insist on asking for lbw. Although they are not in a position to have any idea on the merits of an appeal, they join in the chorus on the basis that if they do not try they cannot get a decision in their favour.

The majority of umpires will agree that they have most doubts when ruling on the tight run-out situations. Here they can be dealing in inches, when the groundsman's markings have been worn away. An additional complication is the confusion that exists with fielders rushing about and inevitably crossing their line of vision.

It is up to the umpire to take up the correct position from which to make the best possible judgement. Normally I move to the side of the wicket on which the ball has been played so that I can see exactly how the bowler or fielder has taken the return. It is up to me to ensure that the wicket has been broken in the proper manner, for it is easy for the stumps to be kicked over or disturbed before the return comes in from the field.

When the ball goes to extra cover or wide midwicket, however, it is safer to move to the other side. This way I avoid getting in the way and, equally importantly, do not get hit on the back of the head by the throw.

There are two golden rules: if in doubt, it is not out; and never try to compensate if you realize you have made an error. Nothing can put it right, and it does not make sense to try and correct one mistake by deliberately making another. I would advise any budding official to concentrate on the next delivery whatever has occurred, for that is the most important thing.

The good umpire has five qualities – honesty, concentration, application, dedication and the calm confidence to inspire and retain the vital respect of the players. A thick skin also helps and I always think it is sad when umpires lose their enthusiasm for the job because they are hounded by players. This applies at all levels and I would remind cricketers that, with very few exceptions, umpires are strictly impartial.

Umpiring in Test matches is especially demanding. The officials have to report to the ground before 4.30 pm on Wednesday – the day before the game starts – to check with both the local secretary and the ground authority.

Personally, I have always been an early riser and I like to be up and about by 6.30 am, so I am on duty by 8.30 most days, making sure that all my equipment is in order in the umpires' room. Although I will have had a talk to the groundsman on the Wednesday, I make a point of having another word as he completes his preparations on the morning of the match. Much of my routine is designed to ease the tension, but I always experience a few butterflies and have to pay several visits to the toilet. For all that I have a lot of experience now, I invariably get caught up in the excitement which builds steadily.

My little mannerisms give away the fact that I am highly strung. As a player my hands were occasionally shaking so much that I had to have help in putting on my pads and gloves. Indeed, it was not unknown for me to walk to the wicket with the gloves on the wrong hands and, since they were the old-fashioned type with the wrap-round thumb, it was almost impossible to switch them over. It must have looked sometimes as though I had broken bones in both hands.

This is why I pay particular attention to the routine checks, which include confirming that the markings are all in order. Umpires do not make too much show of these, though, as the groundsmen are professional men, well aware of what is required. Still it is as well to be sure that the boundary ropes are in the correct place and that the sight-screens function properly.

After enjoying a cup of tea, my next job is to change into the uniform. This consists of a short white jacket, dark trousers, white shirt, black tie and white cricket shoes. Other little matters have to be kept in mind, such as whether the bails fit smoothly into the grooves on top of the stumps. Anyone who thinks this is finicky ought to note how often in club matches the bails do not stay in place.

Umpires are also responsible for putting the balls through the gauge that ensures they conform to the regulations and, if the ground authorities have not already done so, we find out from the captains which make they want to use. In first-class fixtures, the fielding side can pick the one they want from the box.

Bird with fellow umpire Bill Alley during the 1980 English season. The objects on the table are the contents of their pockets.

Finally, I go carefully through the items that I carry with me, laying them out on a table to check them off as I transfer them to my pockets. The list, which might appear a bit on the long side, has been built up over the years, and is:

- Six miniature beer barrels, which are used as counters.
- A pair of scissors. These come in handy if the stitching on the ball works slightly loose, while it is remarkable how often a player needs a finger nail trimming. At Old Trafford in 1974 I snipped the hair of India's Sunil Gavaskar, who was having problems because it kept falling down into his eyes.
- A penknife. This is for cleaning the dirt out of spikes.
- A needle and cotton. I have to admit that I am a very poor cook, but I can put in a neat stitch when the need arises and I have done a lot of running repairs on trousers. This can be embarrassing when they split in sensitive places and I am glad to report that I did not have to do any sewing when I stood in the women's World Cup.
- Safety pins, which are also for patching up little tears.
- A rag for drying the ball.
- A spare bail in case one gets broken, which happens increasingly with so many really quick bowlers about. I suppose we might carry a stump as well, but to avoid walking stiff-legged with it stuck down a trouser leg, we generally leave one handy by the pavilion or in the groundsman's quarters.
- Chewing gum. This is not only for myself. I calculate that it costs me a few pounds each year to keep the players supplied.
- Spare balls, in case the one in use goes out of shape. There is a box in the dressing room containing a number of balls in plastic bags, labelled to indicate how many overs have been bowled with each. Out in the middle the umpires will probably have three spare balls. I might, for example, have one

nearly new and one which has been used for between twenty and thirty-five overs. My partner would then have one which has gone through fifty to sixty-five overs. Anything in between will mean a trip back to the dressing room and a little discussion with both teams in order to reach agreement over a replacement. We do not always allow a change because bowlers are sometimes optimistic in registering a complaint.

I also carry a copy of the playing conditions, which obviously vary from competition to competition. On the domestic scene these are amended at frequent intervals and one change in the 1984 season caused embarrassment for myself and John Holder, the former Hampshire bowler, whose disposition is as sunny as his native Barbados and who is called Benson, after the character in the television series, by the Yorkshire players.

We had been officiating in the Yorkshire v. Nottinghamshire Championship fixture at Headingley and were due in Perth on the next day, when Yorkshire had a Benson and Hedges zonal tie against Scotland. The Headingley game finished late as Yorkshire gained a thrilling victory and, in the circumstances, we had very little time to spare before setting out on the long haul north.

Cricketers are subject to much greater strains than their counterparts in professional soccer, for I can hardly imagine teams such as Manchester United or Liverpool cheerfully allowing their first team to make a late-night dash up the motorway on the eve of an important Cup clash. Yorkshire had no alternative, but to make the best of a bad job they hired a coach and kindly agreed to let the umpires travel with them – in return for a contribution to the cost, of course!

The driver happened to be one of the most cautious men you could meet, maintaining a very steady speed which ensured a smooth ride, but meant that we did not reach Perth until 2.00 am. A friend had arranged to pick me up and take me on to his home for the night, but had clearly abandoned his long vigil ages before we arrived, so I made an emergency booking at the team's hotel and tumbled gratefully into bed.

I have always enjoyed going to Scotland, where you are sure of a warm welcome, and I actually made my first-class debut against the men from north of the border at Hull in 1956. They take their cricket very seriously and have produced some notable performers, including Mike Denness, who captained England.

They are, though, held back by a lack of strength in depth, and Yorkshire, who batted first, held the upper hand. Events were proceeding predictably and quietly in the afternoon and, in accordance with our most recent instructions, John and I brought the teams off for tea after twenty-five overs in the Scotland innings. As we left the field, however, it became clear that neither the officials nor the tea ladies were ready for us.

David Bairstow, the Yorkshire skipper, had also been taken by surprise and we soon discovered why. Scottish official Robin Prentice came up to inform us that we were wrong. 'We have had a letter from the Test and County Cricket Board which states that the tea interval has to be taken after thirty-five overs in the innings of the side batting second,' he pointed out. This alteration, designed to prevent the final session being too long, was understandable, but John and I had not been notified, and the fact that the telephones were a long way away, at the rear of the sports hall which dominated what was a series of playing fields, did not help.

Whatever the arguments, we were off the field and could do nothing about that. The tea interval lasts for only twenty minutes, so we had little room for manoeuvre. As I sat down trying to work out the best course of action, I noticed a very elderly gentleman wearing a heavy overcoat and festooned in a thick scarf picking his way towards me. The tent in which the players were trying to get their sandwiches and which served as a temporary pavilion stood on a small ridge of high ground which ran along the top side of the playing area.

My visitor made slow, determined progress up the incline and, eventually, out of breath and apparently almost ready to collapse, he reached my chair. Pushing forward his hand, he gasped: 'I am ninety-two and have been an umpire in the leagues for more than fifty years. I have always wanted to meet you Mr Bird. You are the best umpire in the world.' Obviously I was flattered by his kind attentions, but my mind was still buzzing with the dilemma caused by the tea interval. 'Thank you very much,' I said and then, without really thinking, added: 'What would you do now?' Unaware of all the confusion, he nodded, smiled and returned the way he had come.

In the end, realising that our hands were effectively tied by some breakdown in communications, we settled for a good old-fashioned British compromize and had two intervals. Play resumed for ten overs after the first, a period in which Scotland, with their concentration presumably broken, managed to score only twenty-two runs, so I imagine it could be argued that Yorkshire gained some slight advantage, but that simply could not be helped.

There was some concern when we came off for the second time and a few spectators, unfamiliar with the details of the Benson and Hedges Cup thought the game was over, but back we went after another twenty minutes for Yorkshire to complete their victory.

During the second interval I went over to the Press tent to explain things, and overheard the local radio representative talking about the day's play in general to cover the hold-up. The studio must have been asking him about the size of the crowd. 'Oh, there'll be three or four thousand here,' he said. This must have impressed them at the other end, for they suggested that this was extremely good for a cricket match in Scotland. 'Aye, it's no bad at all,' agreed the commentator, 'but ye ken, there's been no charge at the gate. It's a free show.'

The newspapers made quite a lot out of the story, although one or two went to the trouble of finding out that other umpires had come off at the wrong time in the previous round of matches. Generally the Press did us a good turn by making it clear that we were in no way to blame. As it turned out, the letters we should have received were delayed in the post and awaited our return home.

I also earned a few headlines in the 1981 season, when fielding restrictions were introduced into the Benson and Hedges Cup on an experimental basis. The idea, picked up from South Africa and Australia, aimed at encouraging more attacking play by preventing sides from putting all their men on the boundary edge towards the end of an innings. It required that, in addition to the bowler and wicket-keeper, four members of the fielding team should, at the moment of delivery, be in an area bounded by two semi-circles based on each middle stump and with a radius of thirty yards. The square leg umpire shouldered the responsibility for keeping an eye on this and had to call 'No ball' if he spotted any infringement.

Arthur Jepson, the no-nonsense former Nottinghamshire seam bowler, was officiating with me for the zonal clash between Derbyshire and Yorkshire at Derby, where play had to continue into a second day when the weather turned sour.

Yorkshire struggled desperately on the Monday as they chased Derbyshire's 202 for eight, and Barry Wood managed to keep a tight grip on their run rate with his very accurate medium-paced seamers from my end. Chris Old, batting with Geoff Boycott, must have noticed that Derbyshire had only three men in the circle, for he suddenly took a huge swing at Wood and had his stumps shattered. Instead of walking, he raised four fingers in my direction and shouted down the pitch: 'I can't be out, Dickie, it was a no-ball. They hadn't enough men in the ring.'

Boycott joined in and I knew they were correct. I had been aware of Derbyshire's error, but under the regulations was powerless to intervene. 'Let's keep calm, gentlemen,' I said as Arthur came across to have a word. 'I think I should have no-balled him,' he admitted. 'I am sure you should,' I replied, 'but what is done is done. We'll have to sort something out.'

'We have far too much to do in the game these days. You need one eye in your backside,' insisted Arthur. The only correct course was to contact Lord's, from where we got a ruling that Old could continue his innings so long as

Bruising barrage – Brian Close hit by a bouncer from Michael Holding, England v. West Indies, Old Trafford, 1976.

another delivery had not been bowled. Old did not profit much, being dismissed almost at once, but Bairstow thrashed a spectacular century – one of the best displays of clean hitting I have seen – to rescue an almost hopeless cause.

It occurred to me that the question of who did what needed looking into, so I raised it with the Test and County Cricket Board. They considered allowing either umpire to take action, but finally decided that the man at the bowler's end had enough on his plate.

Overall, I get on well with all the cricket writers, appreciating that they have a job to do, and I never mind being criticized so long as what is written is fair and accurate. I did, however, demand an apology from Robin Marlar, of the *Sunday Times*, in 1976.

The West Indians had had a ferocious pace attack on duty in the Old Trafford Test and on the Saturday night let fly with a rash of bouncers at Brian Close and John Edrich, who were opening for England. Reports indicated that it got quite dangerous and Edrich was quoted as saying that he had wanted to go off as a gesture of protest. In the *Sunday Times* Marlar wrote: 'Bird stood like a pillar at square leg and did nothing about it.'

He was quite right in stating that I took no action, but that was because I was many miles away, standing in a Championship match in the South. The umpires at Old Trafford were Bill Alley and Lloyd Budd.

I tackled Marlar, who regretted that it was an error in transmission, Bird for Budd. 'Don't worry about it,' he said, but I did worry because he put my reputation on the line.

Just to illustrate how easy it is for the public to get the wrong impression about an umpire, I can recall another Test match incident in which I took a lot of stick for something entirely outside my control. A charity approached me and asked if I could get a bat autographed by the England and West Indies players at Headingley in 1980. I had no engagement, so on the first day I took the bat and went up to Leeds, arriving shortly before the scheduled starting time.

I parked my car and began walking towards the main gates only to be met by a stream of spectators leaving the ground. One of them noticed me. 'You idiot, Bird,' he roared, 'you've ruined our day calling play off this early. You must be out of your mind.' Several others took up the attack. 'You are killing cricket, you fool,' they cried. For a moment I thought they were going to assault me, but, of course, I had nothing whatsoever to do with abandoning play. Alley and Ken Palmer had made what I am sure was the right decision and they were safely out of sight in the dressing room, although I often wonder how it was that the public did not know who they were when they made an inspection.

The question of whether conditions are fit for play is constantly taxing umpires. We appreciate that the public have paid a lot of money to watch games and I am sure that most people will agree that in recent years there has been a big effort to get on with it whenever possible. It is not in the interests of anyone directly connected with cricket to waste time and the often heard suggestion that we prefer to sit in the pavilion playing cards is a long way from the mark.

Indeed, I have stood when it was not really fit and in conditions that would never have been considered fit in the past. For their part, though, the customers must realize that players cannot afford to take ridiculous risks with injury by running and turning on treacherous, wet, slippery grass.

They are, after all, earning their livings. Mike Procter got rather upset with me at Bristol in 1973 during the Sunday League fixture between Gloucestershire and Worcestershire. The ground was soaked, but we talked the captains into giving it a go and Procter opened the bowling for Gloucestershire from my end. He had three wides in his first over. 'I am going round the wicket,' he growled. He did so, but the next ball went even wider. He stood fuming in the middle of the pitch, hands on hips. 'It's impossible,' he insisted. 'You wanted to play, you should have to bowl.'

Things improved as the afternoon wore on and he soon got back his normal good temper. 'They are enjoying it anyway,' he acknowledged with a grin as he pointed to the spectators. 'You were right, we have to offer them value for money.'

The crucial areas are the bowlers' run ups, the covers and midwicket. We do not really take the outfield into the calculations. These days we keep the show on the road unless it is absolutely impossible. The third one-day international between England and Australia in 1977 provides a good illustration.

This took place at the Oval on 6 June, the day before the whole nation switched their attentions to the central feature of Her Majesty the Queen's Silver Jubilee celebrations – Jubilee Day itself. England got to 242 after being put in on a very good batting pitch, with Dennis Amiss contributing 108. He and Mike Brearley put on 161 for the first wicket in thirty-eight overs, but the rest of the innings got caught up in a bit of a panic, with too much big hitting and not enough thoughtful pushing of the ones and twos.

Australia might have been influenced by the unfavourable weather forecast, for in rain-affected circumstances the side batting second can gain an advantage if their innings is shortened and the result is determined by scoring rates. To balance this , they can face poor light, as happened at the Oval.

We were off for an hour when pouring rain broke over the ground with their reply still in its formative stages and many of the spectators went home assuming there could be no further play. Ken Palmer, the other umpire, and I had agreed a plan of campaign with the captains, however. With so much happening on the next day, Brearley and Greg Chappell indicated that we would get through come what may.

As soon as it stopped raining we were back on, but how we managed I will never know. The rain came back with a vengeance and there was a blindingly low sun at the Vauxhall End to complicate life even more for the batsmen. Pools formed all over, but despite everything, the standards were incredibly high. Derek Underwood got through his allocation of eleven overs for twenty-one runs and also captured the key wicket of Doug Walters, but nothing could shake Chappell.

With water dripping from the peak of his cap, he remained in total control. 'It's easier for me than them,' he told me. 'The bowlers can hardly hold the ball and the fielders are sliding all over. We shall win if we stick it out.' And so they did – by two wickets, with Chappell finishing on 125 not out to collect the Man of the Match award from Peter May.

I popped my head round the door to congratulate him as he sat in the bath and he said: 'I reckon the only difference between in here and out there is that the water in the bath is hot.' How right he was. My kit was a soggy mass and my

feet had been soaked for hours in shoes that needed peeling off. I don't know if top-class cricket has ever been played in worse weather, but if it has, I'm glad I didn't have to take part.

Once, in an unguarded moment, I told a journalist, who was criticising us for not playing at a particular time that we would stand in snow if that is what the players wanted. He is not slow to remind me of this, but although he is joking there have been times when I have more or less fulfilled that pledge.

There was, for instance, the Derbyshire-Lancashire match at Buxton in 1975, when snow left a treacherous pitch on which Derbyshire were easily bowled out twice, and the ball played all manner of tricks. More recently, though, we had a blizzard at Leicester at the start of the 1985 season. Yorkshire were the visitors and Leicestershire struggled for runs in their first innings. It was terribly cold and snow began to fall, with West Indian pace bowler Gordon Ferris at the crease.

*Urgent attention –
removing something
from Chris Tavaré's
eye, England v.
Pakistan, Lord's, 1982.*

'Do you want to go off, gentlemen,' I asked. 'I don't know,' he replied. 'I have never seen this stuff before.' In the end we continued and young Paul Jarvis had him caught at the wicket at once. Gordon still seemed fascinated by the weather, but I had tremendous admiration for the people who sat it out and made our efforts worthwhile.

We, after all, were getting paid for our pain. Indeed, I am convinced that the start to the 1985 season was the coldest in my time. I am not a drinking man and would not normally allow even a drop to pass my lips during any match, but things were rather different at the Parks, where Oxford University played Somerset. We all wrapped up in thick underwear and layers of sweaters, but still shivered in the fine, but icy weather. 'I have heard of frozen birds before, but this is silly,' admitted Peter Roebuck. The Somerset twelfth man Brian Rose, taking pity on us from the comparative warmth of the pavilion, produced hot coffee when we had a drinks interval, and I discovered later that he had slipped a small measure of medicinal whisky into the brew.

Bad light causes more aggravation, and I feel we should continue through this, no matter who is bowling. This should be written into the laws and regulations so that the onus is taken off the umpires. At the moment we assess the light with the naked eye and if it is bad ask the batsmen if they want to go off. If they elect to carry on they are allowed one appeal, but the light must have got worse for this to be successful. When play is stopped umpires take a reading on the light meter and do not resume until there has been enough improvement to be measured.

Light, by the way, is not the only problem, and at Scarborough in 1979 we had to consider stopping play because a plague of greenfly descended on the town.

They got everywhere, in your eyes and ears, up your nose and in all your clothing. Middlesex were in the field against Yorkshire and Phil Edmonds bowled with a handkerchief around the lower half of his face gangster fashion.

Umpires, incidentally, have good eyesight – it is checked each year as part of a very tough annual medical which we all undergo. This is absolutely essential since the job is so demanding. I am a fitness fanatic, taking some exercise virtually every day and when I pick up the odd injury Dr Ian Adams in Leeds puts me right. You obviously cannot be mentally alert if your body is tired and aching and I am pleased to say that I have raised a few eyebrows in my time by keeping myself in tip-top condition.

Early in the 1979 season I had Lancashire and Gloucestershire at Old Trafford, where we spent quite a bit of time off the field because of rain. I was chatting with Mike Procter, who I regard as one of the best all-rounders in the history of cricket and second only to Gary Sobers in my own period, and that largely because the brilliant West Indian had the opportunity of competing at Test level. Had Procter had a long international career with the stimulus that world-class competition brings, there would not have been very much between them.

The subject of fitness came up in our conversation and I stressed that umpires had to be just as much on their toes as the players, adding that I spent a bit of time on the road and practising sprinting. 'How do you think you would go on in a race with Andy Stovold?' Procter asked innocently. Not wanting to back down, I replied confidently: 'I think I could beat him all right.' Suddenly the dressing room went very quiet. The fish had been landed.

'Do you umpire another of our games this term?' Procter enquired with a twinkle in his eye that warned me I had been caught. I studied my list. 'Yes, last match of the summer against Northants at Bristol,' I told him. 'Right, I'll tell you what. You can race over fifty yards on the last day of that match and we'll all be there to watch,' he decided as all the players roared with laughter.

I thought very little more about it, assuming that as the days went by they were bound to forget what had been little more than dressing room banter, but when I reached Bristol in September, Procter was waiting. 'Morning, Dickie. Don't forget this one hundred yards race with Andy,' he said by way of a greeting.

There was no way out and my pleas that the original idea involved a fifty-yard dash fell on deaf ears. Interest in the contest grew over the three days and shortly before the end of the game, the Gloucestershire club made an announcement over the loudspeaker system. 'Would members of the public please stay behind when the players leave the field as there is to be a race between Andy Stovold and Dickie Bird.'

Gloucestershire's Andy Stovold in action
during the 1977 Benson & Hedges Cup Final.

That brought a great cheer and I am pretty sure that not a soul went out of the ground. On the contrary, as I looked around, it seemed that one or two were actually coming in. The groundstaff marked out the track with flags and it was settled that Stovold should give me three yards start. He also wanted a five pound bet on the outcome.

I am not a gambling man, but at this stage I did not like to show a lack of faith in myself so I accepted the first wager of my life and got down to the starting line.

At the 'off' I put my head down and went as fast as I could, winning by at least twenty yards to the absolute delight of the crowd, who gave me a tremendous ovation as I pulled up, panting but triumphant. 'I've got to hand it to you, you're a lot quicker than we thought,' grinned Procter. I did not take

*Showing the youngsters
– Bird's own batting
artistry.*

Andy's fiver. Proving my point was enough, but I did do a lap of honour round the ground.

Fitness also counted for a lot in 1984. The Test and County Cricket Board ruled that each Championship fixture would involve two days of 117 overs and one, the last, of 110. They did this in a brave attempt to speed up the over rates, having discovered that a system of fines had not had the desired effect. The umpires were really put to the test. I stood in the Essex *v.* Glamorgan match at Southend in July and turned up on the first morning at 8.30. I walked off at the close of play at 8.20 pm so tired that I staggered through the wrong gate and almost finished up in a lake which is adjacent to the cricket field. Had I got into the water I could easily have drowned, I guess, because, being so mentally drained, I do not know whether I would have remembered how to swim.

This was by no means an isolated or exceptional day and all the time play is taking place the umpires are centrally involved. The players usually get some time in the dressing room and they can relax a bit when they are fielding well away from the bat.

The older umpires are not likely to win any races, but they have lively enough minds and keep closely in touch with trends in the game. We have two meetings each year – April and October – to discuss all aspects of our operation and to exchange views and bring up odd incidents.

I also represent the umpires – there are twenty-five of us – on the Test and County Cricket Board cricket committee, so I put forward our opinions and report back on the reaction I get from the most powerful body within the game. One matter constantly exercising the official mind is the increasing tendency for spectators to invade the pitch at the end of a match. This mostly applies to the one-day competitions, but it is a dangerous practice that is going to cause some complications before long.

I was at the Benson and Hedges Cup semi-final between Yorkshire and Warwickshire at Headingley in 1984, when a full house brought fantastic receipts of £79,500 to underline just why limited-overs cricket is so important. The contest reached an exciting climax with Yorkshire needing five runs to win from the last delivery from Bob Willis. Steve Oldham, an old friend of mine from the Barnsley area, swung and missed. People raced onto the field, the players fled and Warwickshire went on to the final. The umpires ruled one leg-bye from that final ball as the batsmen had crossed on their way to the pavilion, but a more interesting point arose.

The laws state that when an outside agency interferes with the ball the batting side shall be awarded four runs. In this case, such a ruling would have left the scores level with Warwickshire still winning because they had lost fewer

wickets. What, though, would have happened if Yorkshire had lost fewer wickets or, for that matter, the same number? As with so many fundamental issues, it is not easy to lay down hard and fast rules. No one wants to encourage supporters to rush on to the playing area at the end to try to influence the result and it may be that at some stage after a pitch invasion the ground will have to be cleared so that one ball can be replayed.

I hope that it never comes to that because it would be so unfair to the players. I trust that people will realize that by running onto the field they are spoiling things for everyone else by distracting the players when they need to be absolutely on their toes. They cannot give of their best if they have one eye on the boundary and one on the dressing room door.

The risk of injury is present in all sports and I have come across some strange ones. Richard Lumb, the very correct Yorkshire opener who came close to playing for England, and who has now gone to live in South Africa, went out for some catching practice one morning at Park Avenue, Bradford.

Time for a playing comeback?

He had been going through a terrible time, dropping catches in the slips and the outfield with embarrassing regularity, so he got down to basics in an attempt to put things right. Graham Stevenson sent him a skier to start with and the luckless Lumb held the ball but broke his thumb in the process.

Another victim was Jim Cumbes, who had a varied career before becoming Warwickshire's commercial manager. In addition to being a useful seam bowler with Worcestershire, Jim was a goalkeeper in the Football League with West Brom, Aston Villa and Tranmere Rovers. In this role he had a magnetic pair of hands, holding fierce shots and headers without trouble from the closest range, but somehow he could seldom hang on to a cricket ball. He remains just about the worst catcher I have seen, despite a genuine desire to improve.

He was bowling from my end at Worcester against Northants when Wayne Larkins pushed forward and lobbed the ball gently back. It was the sort of catch you might throw to a nervous eight-year-old and I said: 'Good luck, Jim,' as he lunged forward, while his team-mates held their breath. I thought he had failed to lay a hand on the ball as it fell to earth, but I was wrong – he had broken a finger as he dropped the easiest chance you could imagine.

Much more serious are the knocks that occur when fielders are perched perilously close at short leg or silly point. They have understandably taken to wearing protective helmets, something that in the early stages caused queries over the laws. Malcolm Nash, batting for Glamorgan against Derbyshire at Chesterfield, hit the ball sweetly from the meat of the bat. It flew to short leg, where it struck poor Phil Russell in the visor of his helmet, which probably saved his life.

Despite this protection, he suffered a cracked cheekbone and some chipped teeth and was rushed to hospital with blood pouring from his face. The ball actually stuck in the helmet and a Derbyshire player pulled it out to claim the catch. I had, though, ruled 'dead ball' as soon as the accident happened and on that basis gave Nash not out. That interpretation received full support from Lord's, who fully discussed the implications of players wearing helmets.

The umpires enjoy a close relationship with the players and, without allowing any of the contacts to affect our judgement, we can have a chat or a joke on and off the field. One amusing conversation involved Andrew Golding, a young left-arm spinner, who is on the Essex staff but who also played with Cambridge University. The match in question was between Surrey and the University at Banstead, where the county had to work their way out of an embarrassing position. This they did through the efforts of Keith Medlycott and Nick Faulkner, who each scored his maiden first-class hundred.

As the runs piled up, I asked Golding: 'Don't you bowl a bit?' He replied: 'I think so, but the captain obviously doesn't.' Eventually, with Surrey over 300, Angus Pollock, the University skipper, called him up. 'I don't think that's a good idea,' he said, 'you'll probably do better yourself.' Pollock did not press the point and Golding added to me: 'That's my chance of a Blue gone, I imagine.' Whatever the reason, he did not play against Oxford University.

We also do a bit of coaching, even if it's only in offering a word of advice here and there, and I have followed closely the progress of Gloucestershire's David Lawrence, after having a hand in his career.

Although of West Indian parents, he was born in Gloucester and is qualified for England, who are looking for strongly-built pace bowlers. Lawrence is definitely quick, but he struggled to co-ordinate his action and I had to warn him for running down the line of the stumps in one match. Graham Wiltshire, the Gloucester coach, had a word with me about this and asked if I could help in putting him right.

We had a spell in the nets and I gave him a few pointers. It was quite some time before I came into contact with him again, but, apart from thinking that his run was a bit long, I thought he had improved a lot.

Most umpires have been first-class cricketers, although there are some, including Don Oslear and Nigel Plews, who have become excellent officials without the benefit of this background. Clearly if you have taken part as a player, you know a few wrinkles, which must help, but I found it difficult in my first season not to get caught up in the play.

Lancashire were playing Hampshire at Southampton in 1970 and Keith Goodwin, their perky little wicket-keeper was batting. He pushed the ball

*Don Oslear grabs a stump as spectators invade the pitch – England v. India
at Old Trafford in the 1983 World Cup.*

through midwicket and ran at once. From square leg I could sense that he wanted two by the way he went about collecting the first, but I could see, too, that he had no hope of beating the throw. Forgetting myself for a second, I shouted: No Goody, no. Get back, there isn't a second.' Ignoring this advice Goodwin failed by a considerable distance to make his ground and the Hampshire side were in stitches as I put up the finger to send him on his way.

The one thing all the umpires I have met have in common is a desire to help. We have a lot to do, but are ready to do more if possible. Without question we see everything that happens and hear a lot more besides which qualifies us to have opinions on players. Umpires could, therefore, help the Test selectors. Selectors cannot be everywhere and Alec Bedser, the longest serving, has told me of the many hours he has put in travelling to see a specific England candidate spend most of the day with his feet up. It is so common when wishing to check on a batsman to find his side fielding, but the umpires suffer no such frustration and could give sound advice.

2

A Cast of Characters

Y OU NEED CHARACTER TO BE AN UMPIRE and there are plenty of characters who have successfully donned the white coat of officialdom. One who did not make much progress, however, was Gilbert Harding, that much-loved and controversial broadcaster. It is not surprising that few people associate him with cricket, for he hated the game. Indeed, he regarded all sport as a waste of energy.

Nevertheless, he was forced into service in a school match in which the masters set themselves to hand out a beating to the pupils. The sports master, who did not like the studious unathletic Harding, contemptuously hammered the youngsters' bowling to the farthest corners of the field and moved majestically towards his century.

In the nineties, he made a slight mistake which allowed the ball to hit his pads. The desperate young bowler shouted an appeal, even though the delivery had been aimed well wide of the stumps. Harding did not hesitate before raising the decisive finger. The outraged sports master snapped down the wicket: 'You were not concentrating Harding, you foolish boy. That could not have been out.'

Unmoved and drawing strength from his brief authority, the reluctant official stood his ground, but, as his elder stalked angrily away towards the pavilion, he piped up boldly: 'Oh yes I was concentrating and you are right, you were not out really.' Harding never did reveal whether he suffered any dire punishment for his cheek, but I imagine that he never umpired in any other school match.

Even so, it would be a mistake to suppose that he is the only man to have made up his mind on factors other than those presented before his eyes. One umpire, good enough to be appointed to a number of Tests, did not for some reason like a particular Surrey batsman. One of my umpiring colleagues, Sam Cook, came on to bowl in one of his early games for Gloucestershire from the umpire's end after the fall of a wicket had brought the batsman to the crease. As Sam handed over his sweater, the umpire said: 'Whenever you hit that chap on the legs appeal.' To Sam it sounded like an instruction rather than an invitation.

The second delivery to the fated batsman turned and lifted to strike the Surrey player, who had pushed well forward, on the shoulder. I can't ask for that, Sam thought, but the sound of the umpire clearing his throat spurred him on. 'How was that?' he inquired in a whisper. 'That's out,' shouted the umpire.

The hapless batsman, hardly able to accept the decision, dragged himself from the middle, urged on his way by the umpire insisting: 'I have given you out, off you go.' To this day, Sam has no idea what had upset this umpire causing him to react so bitterly. Sam, by the way, is one of the most gentle men you will ever come across and had the distinction of taking a wicket with his first ball in first-class cricket, dismissing an Oxford University man called J. O. Newton-Thompson in 1946.

Most umpires, having easy-going natures, do not get rattled and two players who were quite aggressive in their playing days became calm and reliable officials. They were George Pope, of Derbyshire, and Cec Pepper, the Lancashire League professional, who hailed originally from New South Wales and came to prominence with the Australian Services team.

I played against George in the Yorkshire League when he was almost ready to retire. He specialized in big in-swingers and also produced a nasty leg-cutter, which could be unplayable. George continually tested the umpires, appealing for lbw even when he had a very good idea that the ball was going down the leg side. He had in this respect a well-rehearsed technique which often worked.

He buttered-up all the umpires in the league when they turned him down. 'That was a good decision,' he would say or 'You are right, just missing the leg stump I suspect.' Finally the umpire would give him an lbw almost out of sympathy and George would smile knowingly.

Cec had many jousts with officials, who were not always too sure what to make of his leg-breaks and googlies, and he captured many wickets in the league. A forceful bat, he is one of only two men to have hit a ball over the boarding houses at the Trafalgar Square end of the Scarborough ground, 'Buns' Thornton, the father figure of the historic Festival, being the other. Pepper achieved the feat in the first Festival after the Second World War, striking Eric Hollies, the Warwickshire leg-spinner, beyond the beckoning roof tops. He did the trick after being challenged to attempt it by Arthur Wood, the bouncy Yorkshire wicket-keeper, largely because he never turned his back on a reasonable bet. Cec used to address a few well-chosen words to umpires when they failed to agree with his opinions, but once he switched roles he stood for no nonsense himself. I am told, amusingly, that after Thornton had cleared the houses in 1886 word got round that his big hit had landed in Trafalgar Square and a lady of his acquaintance asked: 'Were you playing at Lord's or the Oval?'

Fred Price, who died in 1969 at the age of sixty-six, was regarded as one of the leading umpires of the post-war period. A wicket-keeper, Fred, who represented Middlesex and England, set a record in 1937 when he caught seven Yorkshire batsmen in an innings at Lord's. The story goes that when he arrived back in the pavilion, a lady – perhaps a relation of 'Buns' Thornton's friend – went up to him and said: 'I was so thrilled with your wicket-keeping, I nearly fell over the balcony.' Fred replied: 'If you had madam I would probably have caught you as well.'

He was a fearless umpire between 1950 and 1967 and once created quite a stir when he no-balled Tony Lock, that tigerish Surrey and England left-arm spinner, for throwing in a match against the Indian touring team at the Oval.

Fred became a celebrity when he stopped play between Surrey and Yorkshire on the same ground and sat down because the spectators were barracking.

'This is not my idea of British sportsmanship,' he said. 'Under the laws concerning fair and unfair play I will not tolerate such behaviour. Three times there have been cat-calls just as the batsman was about to play the ball.' Fred remained seated on the grass until the noise subsided. Then he got up and signalled play to resume. If such standards were applied today, some games might never finish.

Dave Halfyard, the former Kent and Nottinghamshire seamer, established himself as another personality on the fist-class list. Like that famous Yorkshire-man Syd Buller, he had a serious car crash in his younger days. He used to drive everywhere in a bubble car and got involved in a collision in the West Country. Though one of his legs was badly damaged, he made a brave comeback and he still fancied his chances against good batsmen in 1977 while actually on the umpires' list.

The explanation for that unusual state of affairs was that in the previous season he had helped Cornwall to qualify for the first round of the Gillette Cup. Cornwall were then drawn against Lancashire and Halfyard received special per-mission to play, bowling well enough to have the 'big boys' worried at one stage.

One of the most popular figures on the circuit used to be Eddie Phillipson, the former Lancashire fast bowler, who went out of the game in 1983. He used to joke about the number of lbws he gave in a season and some of the players called him 'Eddie the Finger'. Whenever we met he ended up talking about the time he adjudged me lbw at Ashby, where, playing for Leicestershire against Derbyshire on a ghastly wicket, I made seventy-nine out of 135.

I tried to lap Derek Morgan behind square leg, missed and departed as Eddie gave me out. I thought it was going down the leg side and later that night said to him: 'I'm disappointed about that one, Eddie.' He patted me on the back and told me: 'Don't worry, lad, you are just one more on the list.' I had to smile, even though I had been looking for a century, which would have been a considerable feat in those conditions. I reached three figures only twice in my career, despite getting into the eighties and nineties a few times, and once I had the misery of being run out on ninety-eight off a no-ball.

Another man who has won and retained the affection of everyone in in cricket was Alec Skelding, who injected a touch of humour into most things. In charge at Lord's during a game between Middlesex and Northants, he saw Dennis Brookes pad up to a delivery which pitched, came back up the hill from the Nursery End and knocked out the off stump. Dennis departed, sadly shaking his head, as next man Jock Livingston, the tough Australian replaced him.

Livingston asked for his guard, looked around, twirled his bat and asked: 'How many balls to go, Alec?' 'Two,' came the reply, 'but if the first is as good as the last, one will be enough as far as you are concerned.'

It is possible to become something of a character almost by accident. My little mannerisms, which have caught the eye of both Press and public, are not calculated to make me the centre of attention. They stem from my nervousness and are quite natural, but they have helped to make me well known. Equally, the headlines have followed me around.

The John Player League fixture between Sussex and Kent at Hastings in July 1984 was shown on television. Perhaps because of this, a young girl came on the field during the Sussex innings in the late afternoon. She must have had the odd drink and refused to go off, insisting on trotting about on the outfield. Chris Tavaré, the Kent skipper, came up for a word with Alan Whitehead and myself. 'We have got to stop her somehow,' he said. 'She could get in the way of one of my fielders at a vital moment or she might get spiked if she is in a collision.'

'There's safety in numbers, let's go down to her together,' suggested Alan. 'You really will have to go and sit down,' he said when we reached her. She giggled and said: 'I'll only go away if you give me a kiss, Dickie.' What could I do? I gave her a big kiss and off she toddled, back to the anonymity of the crowd, while I filled a few extra lines in the reporters' notebooks.

The majority of players have a keen sense of fun and among them Ray East, the left-arm spinner from Essex, is in a class of his own. This is a considerable but well-earned compliment, for amidst the successes of the last few years Keith Fletcher's team have found time for a few jokes. Keith Pont is a leading light, while Graham Gooch is a brilliant mimic of bowling actions, imitating the peculiarities of top personalities magnificently.

Still East remains the star turn. I am sure that had he turned his attentions to the theatre he would have become a brilliant clown. His timing is perfect. He is also a very good bowler and might have represented England had he taken life rather more seriously. 'I ought to get on the telephone to a circus,' he has told me more than once after going through his repertoire of anguished appeals for lbw. It is not unusual to look down and find him on his knees with his hands together in prayer as he pleads for a decision.

While Essex were tackling Glamorgan at Southend in the John Player League, a car backfired and East went down in mid stride so convincingly that, although we all knew he was joking, one or two of us made involuntary moves to help him. Then, at Chelmsford, the drinks interval became a festive occasion with East on twelfth man duties. Instead of soft drinks he brought out champagne and sent the corks flying all over the place.

On the first-class circuit we are all ready to help each other. A great pal of mine is Jack Simmons, the Lancashire off-spinner who has been dubbed 'The Shy Millionaire' after collecting a record benefit a few years ago. Nothing ruffles genial Jack, but he was a bit upset by the fact that he did not get many lbw verdicts in his favour from me. He raised the subject when we happened to find ourselves flying out to New Zealand together on a coaching trip.

I explained that in my opinion he bowled too wide of the crease. 'You need to get much closer to the stumps and keep the ball wicket to wicket before I'll give anyone out lbw to you,' I said. As it happened we were able to spend quite a bit of time together during the winter and I had the opportunity to help him with his run-up and delivery.

Jack, on his part, worked diligently and by the time we boarded the plane home he had completely solved this problem. 'Carry on this season as you have done in the last few weeks and I can guarantee you will get a stack of batsmen out lbw,' I told him as we parted company, although secretly I hoped that I did not get Lancashire in the first weeks of the coming season. No one will be taken aback to learn, however, that when the appointments arrived I noted that I was scheduled for Old Trafford on the opening day of the Championship programme.

It was one of those days when the new ball made little impact and before long Jack got called up into the attack. 'I'll bowl from Dickie's end,' he told his captain. Seeking to postpone the moment of truth, I suggested: 'Better try the other end, Jack, it looks as if you'll get more turn that way.'

'No, I want your end,' he repeated and he got his way. Immediately he beat a defensive stroke and the ball must have come into contact with the pads, for he turned to me with a confident appeal that echoed all over Manchester, accidentally spraying me in the process.

I straightened up, looked him firmly in the eye and said: 'In the first place, Jack, stop spitting. In the second, that's not out because you ran right across my

'Flat Jack' Simmons –
the Lancashire
off-spinner in action
in 1984.

line of vision so I could not see whether the ball would have hit the wicket or where it pitched.' He looked up at the sky in horror as I added mischievously: 'Perhaps you are getting too close to the stumps.' From then on he made sure that he got off the line of the wickets after letting the ball go and I'm pleased to say that we still get on very well.

I have rather more painful memories of a meeting with Dallas Moir, the giant left-arm spinner from Scotland, who has added 'stature' to the Derbyshire attack . Bowling against Essex at Chesterfield in 1983, he dropped short to Ken McEwan, who middled a well-timed pull. When the slow bowlers are on, I like to stand as close as possible at square leg to keep an eye on quick stumpings, so I had little chance to get out of the way. The ball smashed into my right shin and I thought my leg was broken.

Down I went as if hit by a punch to the jaw and the leg ballooned up within seconds. I was in agony and simply had to leave the field for treatment, but when I tried to stand up I could not bear the pain in the leg. I could never have walked all the way to the pavilion, but up came Dallas. He picked me up, cradled me in his arms like a baby and gently carried me to the dressing room. As he placed me on the bench, I tried to thank him through clenched teeth. 'Think nothing of it, Dickie,' he said, waving his hands. 'After all, you did save me four runs.'

Slow left-arm bowlers as a group seem to be funny men, for Phil Edmonds, of Middlesex, is very witty and my old friend Johnny Wardle, like East, has enjoyed a special relationship with the public in his days with Yorkshire and England.

Sadly Johnny died recently, leaving Yorkshire the poorer for his passing. He had agreed to help the county with the coaching of bowlers shortly before his death and there is no doubt he could have passed on many useful hints. Johnny was one of the best professionals I have known.

Intimidation

ntimidation is the problem of modern cricket, there is no doubt about that. Fast bowlers, fitter and stronger than at any other period in the game, are hunting in packs of three or four rather than pairs and they have begun to dominate the game at international level to the point at which too many batsmen are putting the emphasis on physical safety rather than making runs. This cannot be good.

Cricket has always been a peaceful game, with skill being the decisive factor in the battle between bat and ball. In modern times, though, the rewards for winning have increased considerably and it is only to be expected that the players will try harder for victory. The occasional bouncer is a legitimate weapon and it can bring results.

This has been true down the years. As a young Colt with Yorkshire, I made a special effort to get into conversation with Maurice Leyland, that wonderful left-hander who showed his courage in many tight corners for England. Maurice became county coach and knew all there was to know about the game. He firmly believed that dealing with fast bowling was a matter of attitude as well as ability. 'None of us liked it,' he would say, 'but some of us didn't let on.'

Kerry Packer, architect of World Series Cricket.

In the circus atmosphere of World Series Cricket, the fast bowling was uninhibited and it made for some spectacular watching as Kerry Packer tried to attract the cricketing public, but to the real connoisseur the consequences have been hard to bear. Few players enjoy the constant exploitation of sheer pace and there is a real need to preserve the traditional virtues.

I am not sure what action can be taken, for there are snags whatever argument you support. The first step, though, is to accept that all the evidence supports my contention that there are more aggressive pacemen about now than at any other time.

One of the biggest thrills of my childhood was being taken to Sheffield by my father in 1948 to see Don Bradman's Australians, who, by general consent, are accepted as one of the strongest teams ever to take the field. On reflection, however, they had one weakness which might well have left them at some disadvantage in the 1980s, for the support for Ray Lindwall and Keith Miller was limited in terms of genuine speed. Lindwall and Miller formed an exceptional combination, but the Australians would still have been hard pressed against the West Indies, who can keep a battery of hostile bowling going endlessly, giving the batsman no respite.

They would not allow even the matchless Bradman to score three hundred runs in a day. It is not a case of debating whether he could have handled them, either, for batsmen no longer get sufficient deliveries in the hour to score quickly. If you work on an average of around thirteen overs an hour and take into account the number of bouncers and balls pitched wide and short from which making runs is next to impossible, you can calculate simply how difficult it is to keep the scoreboard ticking over. The run-makers today are such as Geoff Boycott, who possesses the patience to build his innings at whatever rate is possible. Other batsmen tend to get out because they take risks.

I know from first-hand experience just how frustrating life can be in these circumstances. I had the doubtful distinction of opening for Leicestershire against the West Indies at Grace Road in 1963 and found it a nerve-wracking experience. The tourists rested Wes Hall and Charlie Griffith, which came across to us as very good news indeed, but they still had Lester King and Gary Sobers around to use the new ball.

King was a very tall fellow and as he prepared to open the attack, he disappeared in the general direction of the pavilion. I imagined for one moment that he had forgotten something and was going to fetch it before we got under way.

I also wondered if he had gone to look for the rest of the team, for, as I gazed about me, I could see only my partner Maurice Hallam and the umpire. Glancing over my shoulder I realized that all the West Indians were organizing themselves in a menacing semi-circle around wicket-keeper David Allan. 'Are you playing with us?' I asked, but received no more that a series of knowing grins in reply. My worst fears were realized as King pounded in, whirled over his arm and swept the ball like a tracer shell over the top of my stumps while I was still in the act of playing forward.

I had taken leg stump guard, which was just as well. I might not have been here to tell the tale had I been further across. Sobers could be pretty lively then, too. Because he had so much style and did everything with a touch of class, people forget that he was a world-class pace bowler who moved the ball late. He bowled me in both innings to end what proved to be several torrid minutes at the crease.

The really dangerous delivery is definitely not the out and out bouncer, which can be either avoided or hooked in comparative safety. I had to give Keith Boyce a final warning during the 1973 West Indies tour and their captain Rohan Kanhai did not take too kindly to that. I gather England were not happy about the short stuff because Bob Willis set about giving the tourists a taste of their own medicine.

I had to have a word with him as well, but Sobers, who was batting at the time, whispered: 'Don't stop him, I can play this all day. If he goes on I'll get a hundred for sure.' Old Yorkshiremen also tell me that Percy Holmes, who partnered Herbert Sutcliffe so effectively in the 1920s and 1930s, would have 'given a shilling apiece for the sort of bowling that modern batsmen complain about'.

Actually most damage is done by the ball that lifts from not all that much short of a length, follows the batsman and reaches him somewhere between his chin

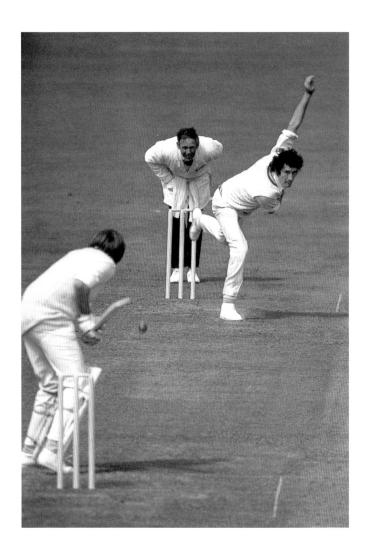

Sussex and England fast bowler John Snow
in his prime during the 1973 season.

and his heart. John Snow, the Sussex and England quickie, could get the ball to fly throat high from almost a good length and worried the best. It takes a lot of skill to survive these and I keep a close watch on them. This type of ball intimidates most batsman and has to be spaced out.

I am always prepared to take a firm stance and have warned a lot of leading performers, including Jeff Thomson, Len Pascoe, Imran Khan, Snow and some of the West Indians who were over here in 1984. That series got off to a bad start when Warwickshire opener Andy Lloyd took a very nasty blow on the head from Malcolm Marshall.

Standing in that game I got the immediate impression that Andy had taken his eye off the ball, a fact he later confirmed, admitting that he had mis-judged the length completely. Marshall went on to bowl three short-pitched deliveries in an over to Paul Downton, all of them rearing unpleasantly, so I asked him to space them out a bit. Worse still, he went round the wicket which indicated to me that he aimed to attack the body and this is a tactic that the West Indians have employed before. Colin Croft, for one, gave Boycott a hard time in this way.

Marshall then tested Ian Botham with three more lifters in an over. Ian, of course, is well able to look after himself, fancies his chances in any company and is ready to chance his powerful arm against any type of bowling. Addition-ally, the laws do make a fine distinction about the batsman concerned, but I still decided to step in. Law 42, which deals with unfair play, lays down the procedure to be followed and states:

Bird watches as England's Andy Lloyd is hit on the head by a ball from Malcolm Marshall, England v. West Indies, Edgbaston, 1984.

> The bowling of fast short-pitched balls is unfair if, in the opinion of the umpire at the bowler's end, it constitutes an attempt to intimidate the striker. Umpires shall consider intimidation to be the deliberate bowling of fast short-pitched balls which by their length, height and direction are intended or likely to inflict physical injury to the striker.
> The relative skill of the striker shall also be taken into consideration.

On balance I decided that enough was enough and that six short-pitched balls in two overs were too many. I called 'No-ball'. I gave Marshall an official warning and, in accordance with the approved practice, informed the square-leg umpire, Barrie Meyer, as well as the West Indian captain, Clive Lloyd.

Marshall, who appeared very upset, promptly kicked the ball towards the boundary. I could not let him get away with that. 'Malcolm, while I am having a word with your captain I would like you to fetch the ball back,' I told him. Lloyd, meanwhile, challenged my judgement. 'This is ridiculous, we are bowling half-volleys,' he claimed, although he allowed himself a half smile when I suggested he must be joking.

Marshall duly retrieved the ball and from that point kept a very full length, being rewarded with a couple of wickets and beating the bat any number of times. The sequel came when I arrived at Old Trafford for the fourth Test. I bumped into Jackie Hendricks, the West Indies tour manager. 'By the way, we are leaving out Marshall because you are umpiring. We don't want him warned again,' he said. Marshall, in reality was injured, having broken a bone in his hand at Headingley, and I am sure he would have played in Manchester if he had been fit.

Another aspect of persistent short-pitched fast bowling is that it can become monotonous for the customers. I appreciate that the sight of a really quick bowler firing away on all cylinders is worth going a long way to see, but there has to be some contrast, something against which to measure the sheer physical nature of pure pace.

Chris Balderstone, the Yorkshire and Leicestershire batsman, who collected two England 'caps' in 1976, made a shrewd observation to me after facing up to the West Indian attack. 'You can be at the wicket for up to half an hour and receive only half a dozen balls off which you might reasonably expect to score. Even when they come between a lot of deliveries that are either well wide or short and lifting and you have only a fraction of a second to make up your mind and go for the attacking shot.'

The spectators might get a handful of strokes in a session and these add up to a poor return on the entrance fee. Another thought that occurs to me is just how hard it is to make your debut against the West Indies. A potential Test career can be held back or destroyed altogether by a hammering at their hands and one or two batsmen have suffered long-term problems as a result of over-exposure to pace and the lifting ball.

There is another side to the coin, for, sparingly used, the bouncer is a wicket-taker. Not in itself, perhaps, but some bowlers have employed it to get the batsman apprehensively on to the back foot ready to take evasive action before slipping in the yorker. That is the traditional recipe for success followed by Fred Trueman, Michael Holding, Dennis Lillee, Andy Roberts, Lindwall and others.

Joel Garner is another who brings variety to his attacking plans. He is certain to get a lot of bounce as he is six feet eight inches tall and lets go from well over nine feet, but his most lethal thrust comes when he spears the ball into the base of the stumps with machine-like accuracy. He picks up wickets galore as the unfortunate victim stabs down too late after expecting one around his chin.

Joel is a very genuine chap. He came up to me at the Old Trafford Test and gave me his West Indian cap, saying: 'I want you to have this to remember me. You are a great umpire.' He did this, remember, after I had warned his pal, Marshall, and his action provided yet another example of the nice things in life which money cannot buy.

I am also concerned about the youngsters who represent the future

Express delivery – Malcolm Marshall bowling during the 1984 Test between England and the West Indies at Edgbaston.

generations of county cricketers. They understandably think that anything the Test stars do has to be right and I have noticed kids playing in the streets hurling down bouncers with their tennis balls. It might not do a lot of harm, but it does not do any good, either, and those with talent will not improve against that sort of background.

A number of ideas have been put forward by influential figures with the best of intentions. One involves drawing a line across the pitch so that any ball landing short of it would automatically be a no-ball. Where, I ask, would it be drawn? The pace and bounce of the pitch is an obvious consideration and what would be all right on a slow surface might be dangerous on something a bit livelier.

Then there is the matter of the bowler. How could the same line apply to Garner and, say, Jonathan Agnew? With the greatest respect to the up-and-coming Leicestershire bowler, he is not in the same class. Similarly the batsmen at the receiving end are likely to have differing abilities and will not, in any event, be the same size. Don't forget, Clive Lloyd and Harry Pilling have made runs together for Lancashire – the one well over six feet and the other barely more than five.

You could not legislate for them and in the final analysis the gains would not be sufficient to justify the means. There has also been a move to

The big bird –
Joel Garner during the
Old Trafford Test
between England and
the West Indies, 1984.

lengthen the pitch to twenty-four yards, its supporters arguing that bowlers have become much stronger and quicker in an era of balanced diets and good, nourishing food. That might create scope for a more even contest between batsmen and the world-class pacemen, but in county cricket and a lot of Tests it is the poor old medium-pacers and the spinners who are struggling to find some response from slow tracks. A glance at the record books will confirm that there are a lot of huge scores and declarations, so, for the majority of cricketers, the pitch is quite long enough already.

Really, the present regulations should be adequate, for there is a well-defined procedure laid down. This states:

In the event of unfair bowling, the umpire at the bowler's end shall:

a) In the first instance call and signal no-ball, caution the bowler and inform the other umpire, the captain of the fielding side and the batsman of what has occurred.

b) If this caution is ineffective, he shall repeat the above procedure and indicate to the bowler that this is the final warning.

c) Both the above caution and final warning shall continue to apply even though the bowler may later change ends.

d) Should the above warnings prove ineffective, the umpire at the bowler's end shall:

i) At the first repetition call and signal no-ball and when the ball is dead direct the captain to take the bowler off forthwith and to complete the over with another bowler, provided that the bowler does not bowl two overs or part thereof consecutively.

ii) Not allow the bowler, thus taken off, to bowl again in the same innings.

iii) Report the occurrence to the captain of the batting side as soon as the players leave the field for an interval.

iv) Report the occurrence to the executive of the fielding side and to any governing body responsible for the match, who shall take any further action which is considered to be appropriate against the bowler concerned.

That gives the umpires a lot of power to deal with intimidation – so long as they are given the backing from higher authority.

One complication, however, is the use of the 'night watchman' – a tail-ender promoted up the order at the end of the day to protect the more likely run-makers among his colleagues. Some bowlers take a considerable pride in doing this job and defend well enough to hang about and annoy the fielding side. Geoff Cope regularly employed a well-organized defence when with Yorkshire, and occasionally prolonged his resistance deep into the following morning.

This is all very well, but fast bowlers do not like this type of situation and tend to treat the 'night watchman' as a specialist batsman. In the first Test between England and Pakistan at Edgbaston in 1978, Iqbal Qasim filled the sacrificial role. Having survived the last few minutes of one day he resumed on the morning of the next and battled away for forty minutes, much to the annoyance of both Brearley and Willis.

The slightly-built spinner whiled away the time between deliveries by telling me that he had taken part in a record partnership in one game back in his native country, and he was obviously pleased at the way he was handling himself when Willis went round the wicket and dug one in at him. My colleague Ken Palmer, standing at the bowling end, took no action so presumably saw nothing untoward, but Qasim took a painful blow in the face and had to retire to have two stitches in his upper lip.

This provoked a storm of protest, with some newspapers seizing on the fact that he had a Test average of only 3.63 in sixteen innings and claiming that he qualified for special protection. Brearley refuted this argument strongly. 'I am very sorry the batsman got hurt, but no more than that,' he said. 'Qasim is a competent player who defended well for a long period. What else do people expect? He had been sent in, after all, to blunt our attack and waste the energies of my bowlers. If our players are sent in as "night watchmen" they realize they will be treated as batsmen. It is difficult to say who is recognized as being able to defend himself and who is not. Cricket is a dangerous game and when you take a bat in your hand you take a risk. I do not see any reason to apologize.'

He made a fair point. These days there are very few mugs with the bat and the vast majority of cricketers fancy their chances of chipping in with the odd runs, so it is basically a matter of keeping a sense of proportion and dealing with each individual case on its merits. I repeat that at Edgbaston Ken Palmer said nothing to either Willis or Brearley and he is a much respected official.

Sometimes a bowler can be carried away in his efforts to serve his team. In the John Player League game against Essex at Southend in 1984, Glamorgan's Winston Davis suddenly peppered Keith Fletcher with a string of bouncers.

In these limited-overs contests, umpires have to signal wide if the ball passes over the head of the striker when he is standing upright, so it was an expensive outburst. As the Essex captain ducked and looked distinctly puzzled, I shouted from square leg: 'What are you doing? Cut it out.' Davis was suitably repentant. 'Sorry, it was just a mental block,' he said and carried on bowling normally.

Bowlers react differently to a warning and some are really fired up by a cautionary word from the umpire. Steve Malone, who has partnered Marshall in the Hampshire attack, said, when I warned the West Indian, that I had done England no favours. 'It means that he will be even more determined in future,' he added. 'Malcolm is at his meanest when annoyed and no Englishman knows him better than me. He is a really friendly guy off the field, but he has two completely separate characters once you put a ball in his hand. Then his only aim is to get the batsman out.'

I cannot, however, worry about what the bowler thinks or I would never do the job properly. Another paceman who took a warning to heart was Sarfraz Nawaz, the more than useful Pakistan seamer. We had an exchange in 1982, when India and Pakistan were twin tourists.

Sarfraz took it into his head to bounce Les Taylor, the Leicestershire number eleven at Grace Road. As the batsman pointed an accusing finger at the bowler, I stepped in and informed the Pakistani: 'That's your short one for this over.

Nightwatchman Iqbal Qasim is hit in the face by a bouncer from Bob Willis, England v. Pakistan, Edgbaston, 1978.

David Lloyd watches as Pakistan's Sarfraz Nawaz bowls during the One Day International between England and Pakistan, The Oval, 1978.

I don't want any more.' Sarfraz was out of line, but the next day he gave the Press an interview in which he tried to justify himself. 'Everyone will be playing in kid gloves in the Test matches between England and Pakistan and England and India this summer,' he said. 'The laws are now ridiculous. The delivery I bowled at Taylor was fair enough. He made it into a bouncer by ducking into it.

The situation now is loaded against fast bowlers and cricket is going soft. If a batsman cannot handle a few short balls he should not be playing.'

Sarfraz could, in fact, bat well enough to look after himself, but that was hardly the point. The law about intimidation is in the best interests of the game. Sarfraz did not bear a grudge and we continued to exchange social pleasantries whenever we met. The conversation usually ended by Sarfraz telling me: 'Oh, Dickie, I am in dispute with the Pakistan Board.' That appeared to be a permanent state of affairs.

I came face to face with hostile bowling as a player, notably when I took a sickening crack on the jaw from Frank Tyson, who is ranked among the fastest of all time. Hampshire's Butch White also had me reeling from a blow on the head, while one or two of the top-flight medium-pacers could inflict heavy punishment.

Leicestershire and Essex did battle on a very fiery wicket at Ilford in 1961, when we crashed to defeat by 207 runs. On a bone-hard, fast surface the seamers operated throughout and you needed a bit of luck to avoid taking a knock or two. Trevor Bailey and Barry Knight, who were not much more than lively, hit me all over my body. I took a fearful battering on the first night and another one in the second innings when we chased an impossible target of 347. I ended up black and blue down my left side and could hardly walk as I left the dressing room.

Still I had got in line and had no reason to regret my part in the proceedings, particularly as Maurice Hallam, my captain and opening partner, had scored sixty-nine runs in two innings to my thirty-two, mostly by making room and slashing the ball into the area wide of gulley. 'That was a magnificent effort of yours,' said Bailey. 'I'm not so sure,' I replied. 'Maurice got twice as many runs by backing away.'

Never mind that, yours was the real innings,' he insisted, but I have reflected since as I have watched players flat-bat the ball high over slips that the correct way is not necessarily the right way. Tony Greig also made a lot of runs by giving himself room and I have heard others defending that sort of approach. It's a funny game sometimes.

It looks it when you see so many batsmen in protective helmets. They have become part of the scenery to such an extent that special provisions are made for storing them and the fielding side use a hole in the ground at Headingley.

Most batsmen prefer to keep them on all the time, reasoning that the more they are accustomed to them the better, even if this results in them being worn against spinners or medium pacers. They afford valuable protection and increase confidence, although they do tend to give the bowlers a bit more licence. After all, if the batsman is protected he can expect one or two short ones.

Lillee and Company

P EOPLE WITH AN INTEREST IN SPORT tend to look back with enchantment. To many of them things always seem to have been better in the past. Obviously we cannot express worthwhile opinions about how good W. G. Grace was, since all our information comes from pictures which hardly flatter him, from jerky old film or from the purple prose of some scribe with little to compare him against. Nor can we say with any conviction that Harold Larwood was a more lethal fast bowler than his modern counterparts. Having had the best possible vantage point from which to study today's top stars at close quarters, I am sure that the majority would have been outstanding in any generation.

Some of them have gone right through their careers while I have been umpiring and I can clearly remember players such as Dennis Lillee, Rodney Marsh, Clive Lloyd and Michael Holding as raw recruits. From the start they revealed an eye-catching talent, but so much of it was uncontrolled when they first visited these shores.

As a twenty-two-year-old in 1972, Lillee had long hair which blew about all over the place and the ball tended to do much the same. He was quick all right, but did not have all that much idea where he was going to pitch his next delivery and he also ran down the line of the stumps a lot, getting a few lectures for his pains.

In the circumstances, the batsmen had to rely on a bit of guesswork as well, so Lillee had the element of surprise working in his favour. When he got one straight it often counted. Gradually gaining useful experience in the Lancashire League, he learned to harness his abilities until he developed into the best fast bowler of all time, in my opinion. Without doubt he is in a class of his own among contemporaries and I cannot imagine that there have been any better among those who have gone before. I rate Fred Trueman highly, but not quite so highly as Fred ranks himself, and we debate that issue whenever we meet.

Both Lillee and Trueman had the benefit of perfect natural actions, which

Raw menace – Dennis Lillee in action,
England v. Australia, Trent Bridge, 1972.

explains why they were able to go on for so long, albeit at a slower pace as the years took their toll. They also earned reputations for getting into trouble with the authorities.

I can put my hand on my heart, however, and say that I never had any bother with Lillee, who behaved like a gentleman whenever I had dealings with him. As a true professional, he competed very hard, giving no quarter – as do all Australians and Yorkshiremen, for that matter – but I discovered that if you treated him properly you got an immediate friendly response.

The well-publicized incident of Lillee's metal bat is a neat illustration of just how easily things can get out of hand. Because of Lillee, the first Test against Mike Brearley's 1980 England team in Perth had to be held up while he

Trying it on –
Dennis Lillee wearing
Bird's cap during the
Test between England
and Australia,
The Oval, 1981.

defended what he saw as his right to use an aluminium bat which he was marketing. Brearley's claim that it damaged the ball, thus changing the balance of the contest, won the day. Lillee promptly hurled the bat some fifteen yards, starting a scene and earning a reprimand.

The English Press wrote some strong articles claiming that he had got off lightly, but I know he regretted what happened without accepting that he had been entirely to blame. I happened to be in Perth and had a drink and a chat in the Australian dressing room, where Lillee showed me the bat and explained his plans to encourage its development and commercial exploitation. 'I checked with all the authorities and they agreed that there was nothing in the regulations to prevent my using the bat,' he said. 'I don't know why they have changed their minds.'

Lillee also told me that independent tests had indicated that the ball suffered no extra damage and he still has faith in the project. The traditional willow is getting more and more expensive, so perhaps his bat will reappear at some time in the future.

During the Oval Test in 1981 the sightscreens got stuck making it difficult to adjust them. Despite the endeavours of the public and the man in charge, they refused to budge. I decided to go and supervise the whole business myself, but as I set off, Lillee came running up, snatched my white cap, and shouted: 'Leave it to me, mate, you have enough to do out in the middle.' Much to the delight of the crowd, he got the sightscreen sorted out to the batsman's satisfaction, but not without a good deal of arm waving that reminded me of a conductor at the Royal Festival Hall.

Lillee has a very keen sense of humour and he inspired a very successful practical joke at my expense at the Old Trafford Test of 1981. I got ready in the normal way, checked all my bits and pieces and prepared to leave the umpires' room for the field. Suddenly I heard a commotion in the doorway and some Australians pushed their way in, so, after ushering them outside again, I decided to make sure nothing had been taken.

When I put my hand in my pocket it closed around a curled up snake which I hurled across the floor and ran out, calling to the attendant. 'There's a snake in there. For heaven's sake get rid of it,' I shouted.

Lillee and Rodney Marsh were very perky throughout the first session, asking me if everything was all right and insisting that I looked a little out of sorts. I said nothing, but got on with the morning's play and put the matter out of my mind, hoping that the intruder had been rounded up by the authorities. Nevertheless I was very apprehensive when we reached the luncheon interval.

I was ready for a break, if only to steady my nerves. The soup bowls were already on the tables when we arrived in the dining room and they had little metal covers to keep the soup warm. I lifted mine without thinking and there, still curled up, was the snake again. The speed I produced to win my bet with Andy Stovold at Bristol had nothing on the turn of foot I displayed in clearing the danger zone. Sweat was pouring off me when I reached what I imagined was the safety of the corridor. I could hear the roars of laughter behind me and finally I had to join in as Lillee came after me to explain that the snake was made of rubber. I could have sworn it was the real thing.

Lillee has also shown me a lot of kindness. After the Centenary Test at Lord's he gave me his special white cap, which he signed: 'To Dickie with best wishes.' I received another gift at the conclusion of the short Australian tour which came at the end of the 1975 World Cup. Lillee presented me with a little parcel and said: 'Don't open this until you get home.'

I nursed it all the way back to Barnsley before discovering that it contained an official touring tie with a message which read: 'Going back to Australia with an open-neck shirt. You can have my tie because I think you are a great guy and we all think you are a fair umpire.' Things such as this have convinced me that it is best to judge people as you find them.

Another tough character I have come to regard as a good friend is Rodney Marsh. When he first came into the Australian side they called him 'Iron Gloves' because he had a shaky start and did not always collect the ball in the approved manner, but he had the kind of courage that enabled him to overcome all obstacles. I suppose of all the players I have met, Marsh must be the most competitive – you can almost feel how much he cares when you are out in the middle. Like Lillee he has never stopped working at his game and I put him in the same company as Keith Andrew, of Northants, Wasim Bari, the athletic little Pakistani with a beautiful pair of hands, Alan Knott and Bob Taylor.

Marsh never knows when to give up and no cause is altogether lost while he is in there fighting. I remember when he played Test cricket with a broken toe and I had to ask him: 'Are you all right, Rod?' 'I will be if we win.' he replied. He has contributed more than his fair share of runs to Australia's late order, being at his best under pressure, when he is very well aware that it is up to him to pull the side out of trouble.

Concerned about the weather, Bird with fellow umpire David Constant and captains Ian Botham and Greg Chappell just before the start of the Centenary Test, England v. Australia, Lord's 1980.

Opponents have a healthy respect for his fighting qualities and are relieved to see his back. Interestingly, both Lillee and Marsh admire the matching determination of Geoff Boycott. In the Centenary Test at Lord's, persistent rain virtually ruled out a positive finish, but Australia, having piled up 385 for five before declaring, broke through by dismissing Graham Gooch and Bill Athey cheaply. Boycott, however, survived Lillee's ferocious burst, and, as he did so, the bowler muttered; 'If I could only get rid of him, you would be on your way home early.' Boycott, of course, held things together in his usual calm way.

Lillee's most famous partner was, unquestionably, Jeff Thomson and together they blasted Mike Denness and his men to defeat in the 1974–5 series in Australia. They were unplayable and, cracking a few bones in the process, undermined the foundations of one or two careers.

David Lloyd, the Lancashire left-hander, with a well developed sense of self-preservation, went out of his way to be nice to Lillee, and was heard to ask more than once, doubtless with tongue in cheek: 'Do you want to borrow my car tonight, Dennis?' or 'Is there anything I can get you?' Imagine his horror, then, when Lillee, while batting, got some short stuff from Tony Greig, who actually hit him a nasty blow on the left elbow. Words passed between these abrasive characters and Keith Fletcher, from gully, called out: 'Well bowled Greigy, let him have another one.'

Careless talk, they say, costs lives and Lloyd, knowing that he had to face Lillee eventually with the new ball, stepped in as peace maker, offering to massage the tender spot. As it turned out his labours were not in vain, but Fletcher walked into a hurricane. Lillee went flat out against the diminutive

Essex captain and one wicked delivery leapt up and hit Fletcher right on the cap, where the tour badge of St George and the dragon proudly perched. Down he went and Geoff Arnold, watching the drama unfold from the dressing-room window, groaned: 'Good Lord, he's knocked old George off his horse, now.'

Lillee remained a fiery handful, despite having a bad back for much longer than most people realize. As far back as 1972 he admitted to me: 'I am in agony sometimes.' You have to take off your hat to the man who refused to give in to pain. He followed the advice of Dr Frank Pyke, a lecturer in physical education at the University of Western Australia, and trained for at least two hours three nights each week.

In addition to pounding the streets for three and four miles at a time, he subjected his body to a complicated system of exercises, so anyone who thinks that being a fast bowler is fairly easy should give Dennis a ring. I advise them to keep the ear piece at a safe distance.

That, of course, is where Lillee is so different to Trueman, for I never heard of Fred being on the physio-therapist's table in all the years he played. He was lucky to have such a superb physique which stood up so well to the strains of his profession.

Two other Australians with whom I have enjoyed a good relationship are the Chappell

Talking tactics – Ian and Greg Chappell during the Fourth Test, England v. Australia, The Oval, 1975.

brothers, Ian and Greg. Greg has so much talent and is as good a stroke-player as I have seen. He is credited with many Test match centuries, but I can think of nothing better than the ninety-nine I watched him make for the Australians against Somerset at Bath in 1977. Coming in at the fall of the first wicket, he had a century there for the taking in the first session, but for some reason he quietly steered his way through a maiden over – the last before the interval – apparently unaware of the scoreboard.

Facts and figures mean very little to him. He announced his retirement from
Test cricket before the fifth Test against Pakistan in Sydney in 1984 when he still
needed sixty-nine runs to overtake Don Bradman and become the highest
scorer for Australia. He thus ran the risk of not earning a place in the history
books and could justifiably have waited to see how he got on in that match.
Typically he thrashed the Pakistan attack to reach 182. For good measure he
caught Mohsin Khan when the tourists batted again, thus beating Colin
Cowdrey's total of 120 Test catches.

Greg has no superiors as a batsman, and I place him right at the top in the
same category as Viv Richards, Clive Lloyd, Barry Richards, Zaheer Abbas,
Graeme Pollock, Rohan Kanhai, Sunil Gavaskar and Gordon Greenidge. All
of them make batting look almost too easy. The strokes involve little effort
and it is impossible to believe the ball has been hit so hard until you see it
racing to the boundary leaving helpless a fielder with only a yard or so to make
to cut it off.

There is real pleasure to be had in watching them, but if I had to back a man
to play a long innings to save my life I would look no further than Boycott, who
has dedication and application to spare. He never tires of saying: 'Dickie, Test
matches are won by batsmen who play long innings,' and his is the wicket the
bowlers prize the most.

Kanhai played alongside the three Ws – Frank Worrell, Clyde Walcott and
Everton Weekes – but when discussing outstanding performers he shook me by
saying: 'You know, on all pitches I believe Peter May to be the best.' That is high
praise indeed.

Walter Hammond is my selection as just about without equal on all pitches. I
had the privilege of seeing him when I was a boy and the stories of his exploits
are amazing. Although they read like chapters from some schoolboy serial,
most of them are true. Sam Cook never tires of describing a partnership with
Hammond which added sixty for the last Gloucestershire wicket. Sam marched
out as number eleven to join the great man, who already had a century to his
credit. Sam never had to face a single delivery as the runs flowed from the other
end. Lancashire, increasingly desperate, went to great lengths in their efforts to
get at Sam, but Hammond contemptuously got his single off the last ball of
each over.

Arthur Jepson also got a close look at Hamond in full cry. Bowling for
Nottinghamshire, he took some fearful stick. Charlie Barnett thrashed a
glorious ninety-nine before lunch, inspired by an argument with Hammond,
and called out loudly as he reached the pavilion: 'That's how to bat, Wally.' Poor
old Arthur plugged away through the afternoon as Hammond hit a double

century between lunch and tea before strolling off to reply: 'No, that's how you bat, Charlie.'

Another masterly display came at Bristol, where, after a Hammond century, Tom Goddard bowled out Somerset twice on a turning pitch. Some discussion prompted Hammond to prove a point, so out he went to the middle and on the same pitch comfortably kept out Goddard using only the edge of the bat. The others could only stand and admire his flawless technique.

To return to Greg Chappell, one other facet in his make-up was his admirable temperament. He never lost his cool, whatever the circumstances. Amidst great excitement he jogged along, concentrating on his own game and serving his side all the better for that.

All the same, Greg permitted no liberties to be taken and the same applied to Ian, who, while not so gifted as a player, earned a tremendous reputation as a captain. He is among the four I respect most for their all-round knowledge of the game and its subtle tactics, the others being Richie Benaud, Ray Illingworth and Mike Brearley.

Ian, with a keen eye for the main chance, admitted: 'You are for ever learning things as a captain and I used to buy Ray a pint of lager just so I could sit and talk to him about cricket. He knows so much you can't help but pick up tips even in the most casual conversation.' That's true enough, but being very much a Yorkshireman Ray would not give much away on the strength of one drink and I bet he carefully rationed his advice.

Brearley had a knack of doing the right thing almost by instinct and all his team-mates regarded him in awe. In part they were influenced by his university background and his formidable educational qualifications, but he had a special air of confidence about him which had an effect on the opposition, too.

Benaud is just about the nearest thing there has been to a perfect captain, because he not only studied every aspect of the game but also understood human nature. He persuaded his bowlers that they could get wickets in the most unlikely circumstances and generally had a trick up his sleeve to help give them an edge. If you listen to his comments on television you will understand how he came to be such a success. He spots odd almost insignificant points which are, in fact, important, and I would bet that there is not a single cricketer in the world who would really challenge his opinions.

Down the years I have observed many captains and the job simply bites into their careers. With so much responsibility, especially at Test level, it is staggering that they manage to pick up a few runs and wickets. The leader of any side is involved with selecting the eleven, ensuring that his men are reasonably happy and making all the decisions. There are plenty of discussions, but in the end someone has to grasp the nettle and it is small wonder that individual form has to be sacrificed. A good captain has to put personal achievement a long way down his list of priorities, and, on top of all this, he knows criticism will descend on his head if his plans go wrong.

There is no shortage of experts on the sidelines and the comments can be heard in the middle. 'He should have been off half an hour ago' – this usually when some bowler has been a bit expensive. 'He ought to have had a man there' – this when the batsman has found a gap to collect four runs, although if you listen long enough you will realize that the average critic uses about fifteen or sixteen fielders.

Captains have to motivate the men around them, even when they are worried about their own problems, and have to note the little idiosyncrasies. One player will need driving, another coaxing and, at the end of it all, the captain has to go before the committee, report on events and justify his actions. In some cases, therefore, a long-awaited and eagerly sought promotion to the 'hot seat' has ended in disaster.

Ian Chappell scored heavily so far as motivation was concerned, giving a hard-headed lead that others followed willingly. He harnessed the explosive talents of Thomson and Lillee brilliantly, which was rather more difficult than might be imagined. The temptation to 'kill' them with too much work had to be resisted, and Ian kept them fresh and keen to have another go. They operated to cleverly set fields, for Ian read the tactical situations well and planned carefully.

I thought Clive Lloyd was a fine captain, but not quite in this group I have mentioned. He had a wonderful record and handled things efficiently. He did a great job for West Indies cricket, but with his endless battery of pace bowlers I reckon the hardest part had to be tossing up. Even I might have won a few Tests as captain of the West Indies, for they could compensate for the odd mistake.

They have been the dominant force for a number of years, with two triumphs in the World Cup competitions and a string of Test victories. Not many teams have got the better of them, but I joined in the cheering when Yorkshire did the trick at Middlesborough in 1963. The tourists beat England by three matches to one, so it was a fine effort by the county, although Doug Padgett and John Hampshire took sickening blows from the fast bowling of Charlie Griffith and my old friend Lester King.

Fred Trueman tells an amusing tale about the return fixture at Sheffield. The West Indians did not like the chill weather of the north-east in May and left Middlesborough warning that when the sun shone later in the summer things would be a lot different. Sure enough, they won by an innings and two runs at

Bramall Lane. Just after lunch on the last day, Yorkshire's second innings lay in ruins. Needing ninety-eight to avoid an innings defeat, they had slumped to seventy-five for five wickets. Wes Hall, Griffith, Sobers and King were in full cry as demolition experts and the walls came tumbling down.

Fred set himself to hold up his end and delay matters as long as possible in the forlorn hope that rain or some other natural intervention would come to the rescue. Griffith, bowling from the football ground end, departed into the distance. 'Is he allowed to have the traffic stopped in the street?' asked Fred when it appeared likely that the bowler might actually start his return journey from outside the ground. Griffith came thundering down his well-worn path, but just as he got into his delivery stride Fred backed away and held up his hand. Griffith screeched to an angry halt. 'I am sorry, but I will have to have the sightscreen moved,' said Fred. This happened to be fastened down and wedged in, so the combined weight of the whole groundstaff was required to complete the adjustment.

Finally the action got under way again and, possibly to get their own back, the West Indians crowded around Fred in a variety of close-catching positions. Once more Griffith trudged back to his mark, turned and came powering his way back towards the stumps. Straining every sinew he built up to top speed only to veer away as Fred backed off again. 'What on earth is the matter now?' demanded umpire Tommy Spencer. 'Well,' replied Fred, 'if this lot do not move back a bit I am going to make an official appeal against the light.' A few minutes later it was all over. Yorkshire lost five wickets for nine runs in seventeen minutes, but Fred still enjoyed his moment.

Getting back to Clive, his powerful hitting of the ball has delighted spectators everywhere, particularly as he has such a lazy style. He is a quiet man who often gives the impression that he is ready to nod off. For a long time he has been telling me: 'This is my last season, I can't go on any longer,' but he keeps coming back.

Holding is another West Indian who has developed so impressively, although he somehow misses out when the plaudits are being handed around, possibly because he is such an undemonstrative figure, rarely drawing attention to himself except through his spectacular bowling. I have nothing but admiration for this smoothly oiled machine who is capable of generating what his country-men call 'pace like fire'.

His outstanding performance at the Oval in 1976 can rarely, if ever, have been matched in terms of speed on an unresponsive wicket. It was a real, old-fashioned feather bed on which you would have backed anyone with claims to being a Test batsman to make runs. Viv Richards put together 291 with such

Who's grovelling now? The West Indies celebrate after Tony Greig is clean-bowled by Michael Holding, England v. Australia, The Oval, 1976.

disregard for the England attack that he looked like someone having a net. West Indies reached 687 for eight before declaring.

England fought gallantly, with Dennis Amiss scoring 203 in his solid, technically correct way. The most significant moment came with Tony Greig's appearance at the wicket. He had been the centre of a controversy from the start of the series when in the course of a Press interview he indicated that his intention was to make the West Indes 'grovel'. It was widely understood that he merely meant that England hoped to take command and crush the opposition, but his words had an unfortunate ring and he became the target for the indignant West Indian pacemen.

Greig did not lack courage and he showed he could take the fight to the enemy by cracking a loose delivery to the boundary. He oozed confidence and the crowd rose to his bravery, but Holding smiled and said to me: 'I can bowl this fellow for a pastime.' This, of course, was the fifth Test and I agreed. 'Michael, I have noticed that throughout the series,' I said.

Being a tall man, Greig had a big back lift and Holding took full advantage. Having watched him despatch a half-volley with a full swing of the bat, he whispered: 'This one, Dickie.' I crouched down and Holding came up to deliver a ball that was just as fast as the one that bowled Boycott during the often described 1981 Test in Bridgetown.

On what he regarded as a less than perfect pitch at the Kensington Oval, Boycott had his offstump plucked out of the ground by a 'rifle bullet' and collected a 'duck' of which he is not ashamed. Greig equally had no reason to be self-critical. By the time he got his bat down the middle and leg stumps were dancing beyond Deryck Murray.

The West Indian fans responded with jubilant celebrations and flooded onto the field. For the first time in England a Test match was halted by a crowd invasion and we just had to try to protect the pitch. One huge chap came straight up to me. 'Are you Mr Dickie Bird, professor of cricket?' he asked. 'That's me,' I answered, trying to humour him. He produced a roll of notes and peeled off fifty pounds in five pound notes. 'Give this to Michael Holding for bowling that Greig man,' he instructed.

I stuck it in my back pocket and continued to help in restoring order, forgetting about the money until after the close of play. Being unable to contact Michael Holding, I put it to one side and eventually, like a good Yorkshireman, took it to the Halifax Building Society...and it's still there if the West Indian pace bowler ever wants to claim it! I am not a great one for statistics, but I made a note of Holding's figures in conditions that gave him no assistance.

He claimed eight for ninety-two in the first innings, when Andy Roberts had none for 102, and six for fifty-seven in the second – fourteen wickets for 149 runs. If you study the scorecard you will notice as well that twelve of his victims were either lbw or bowled, which proves he kept the ball well up and got his success through skill alone.

Holding maintained an amazing accuracy and put his trust in sheer pace. He has such immaculate control that he is no problem to the umpires, rarely over-stepping. Along with Malcolm Marshall he has such an athletic run that you cannot hear him coming up to the stumps. Some pacemen announce their arrival with pounding feet and heavy breathing, but not this super smooth pair. They are just like ghosts and hardly leave a mark on the field in the course of their run-up.

CHAPTER 5

Neutral Umpires

Sit down please! Bird during the First Test between England and New Zealand, Trent Bridge, 1990.

A YOUNG AND NERVOUS RECRUIT to county cricket once asked Frank Chester, the legendary umpire who set the standards for all those who came after him, if it was true that he gave the benefit of the doubt to the batsman. 'Doubt,' exploded Chester, shrivelling his questioner with a piercing glance, 'when I am umpiring there never is any doubt.' I did not have the pleasure of seeing Chester in action, but I will not accept that he never made a mistake or that he thought he was perfect, either. In his long career he gave thousands of decisions and some of them must have been marginal. That is the nature of the business.

We are dealing with inches and fractions of seconds and are bound to fall into error at some time or another. What it is important to realize, however, is that umpires all over the world are honest men doing their best in difficult circumstances, without fear or favour.

This is why I am basically against the idea of creating an international panel to handle Tests, because there is no guarantee that such a move would end all disputes. It is a nice idea in theory, but once you get down to discussing the practical side the queries keep cropping up. David Constant, who has a lot of experience at the highest level, agrees with me. We have discussed the whole issue often enough and he is certain, too, that bias does not play any part in the majority of umpires' rulings.

He sums up his opinion like this; 'I would be unhappy to see overseas umpires standing in Tests in England if I knew there were better qualified Englishmen ready to do the job. I think the players would argue this way also. It might be worthwhile compiling a list of the best men, irrespective of their country, rather than sticking to the point of umpires being neutral in geographical terms.

The feeling throughout the cricketing world, though, tends to favour neutral umpires, with a lot of international captains lending their support. Clive Lloyd, Greg Chappell, Sunil Gavaskar, Imran Khan and New Zealanders Jeff Crowe

and Geoff Howarth have all voiced strong criticisms of the present system, and have also hit out at standards when on tour. So there is influential backing for the panel idea.

Usually, the argument is that umpires have favoured the home team and public accusations have brought tensions to the big matches, thus adding to the burdens of the men in the middle, who, in some cases, have been in genuine physical danger after upsetting local heroes. This, I am convinced, has become a very important matter. Captains are too ready to talk to journalists, who seldom need much encouragement to over-dramatize things.

The fact that captains express themselves so forcefully leads to striking headlines which inflame the passions. There is a proper channel through which they can bring their comments to the attention of officials, and captains should confine their remarks to these reports. By doing so they would avoid unpleasantness. Relationships on the field must be strained if umpires suffer the embarrassment of being attacked in public, particularly when, however politely it is wrapped up, the charge is cheating.

Each decision can become a test case if people are not careful, with players appealing for just about everything and looking astounded when they are turned down. I cannot state too strongly that I have never come across an umpire who gave other than a fair judgement.

The tradition of trusting the home country's officials has given cricket a special standing. I chat with quite a few soccer referees during the winter when I pop down the road to watch Barnsley and they are all impressed by the way umpires are so readily regarded as being impartial. The Football League takes pains to avoid the charge of favouritism by appointing independent referees, and even that bastion of amateurism and sportsmanship, Rugby Union, follows a similar line, yet referees rarely make decisions of such crucial significance as umpires.

In England, of course, we are nearly all former players with well documented county connections, but when we are umpiring we see only the batsman, the bowler and the fielders. As far as I am concerned, they might just as well be robots, for I shut out of my mind all knowledge of who they are or who they represent. As I assess a situation, all the personalities involved become anonymous. I can, therefore, say that while I am very proud of having represented Yorkshire and Leicestershire, I give decisions for and against my old counties without the slightest thought for the individuals concerned.

One night at Northampton I stayed in the Abington pub, which is just down the road from the ground, and swapped stories with some of the Northamptonshire lads. Predictably I got round to Yorkshire, who were taking part in the match, defending them against some good natured ribbing and proclaiming that they were still the best county in the world.

A customer tugged my arm and said; 'I don't think you should be so loyal to one side when you are standing in the match.' I looked him straight in the eye and put him right. 'Don't worry,' I told him. 'In here I am a Yorkshireman, out there I am an umpire. That's the difference.'

As I understand it – and it is important to realize that up to now no one has put forward a concrete plan – the international panel would be formed by inviting a group of Test umpires to make themselves available on a full-time basis. They would then, presumably, be assigned to various series, but, whichever way it is organized, I see snags cropping up, even though I would be honoured to be chosen.

In the first place, how would these umpires be picked? Is it the intention to give all the Test-playing countries equal representation? Without pushing my own claims or those of my English colleagues, it is fair to say that we maintain comfortably the highest standards. It would, therefore, be wrong to leave out some excellent umpires from England to accommodate less well qualified men from elsewhere because this would mean a decline in the level of competence.

It is surely no use having neutral umpires if they slip up because they lack the necessary background. Indeed, home crowds are not going to be very tolerant of a 'foreigner' making mistakes, particularly if they happen to prove costly to their side.

This applies particularly to the 1987 World Cup in India which is a special case. The Test match situation involves different problems.

To illustrate the dangers, suppose an English umpire happened to get it badly wrong at the expense of the Australians in Sydney. The Hill is not the most philosophical place in the world and the odds are that the reaction would be swift and explosive, with the neutral umpire becoming a 'cheating Pom' in their eyes.

Another factor relates to the possible removal of incentives for umpires making their way up the ladder. At the moment, most officials have Test matches as their target and they work steadily towards this goal. Some would lose interest when they realized that promotion prospects had been strictly limited by the fact that their country's quota on the panel was full.

Then there is the expense to take into account. Three umpires represent the minimum requirement for a full series, since two could not hope to cope with all the games. Some Tests are now 'back to back', with only a day in between, and the programmes are packed with one-day internationals as countries try to squeeze the maximum profits out of a tour. Umpires would have to receive generous travelling, hotel and meal expenses, not only during the matches, but while they were resting. Add their fees and you come up with a sizeable sum to reduce some of those profits.

I am not sure either that these neutral umpires would cope with the atmosphere on the various Test grounds. I regard Test cricket as a very big occasion, matched possibly only by the Olympic Games. It can be hard to settle down when you are on familiar soil, so the problem is certain to be much bigger for strangers.

Also, I cannot see there could be any improvement in England – a theory not based on any misplaced sense of national pride, but simply because our crowded domestic routine and the way in which we operate equip us for anything. English umpires are in action seven days a week and are gradually brought to the stage at which they can handle pressure and tense situations. In other countries this method, allowing for steady, controlled promotion does not apply.

As a consequence you can get some relatively raw recruits stepping up to handle top-level games. In the final match of the 1978–9 series between Australia and England 'down under', for example, Don Weser and Tony Crafter were both taking part in their first Test. As England swept to an overwhelming victory by nine wickets, a disagreement arose over the laws. Australia used an old ball from the start of England's brief fourth innings because the pitch allowed some turn and they relied on spinners Bruce Yardley and Jim Higgs.

Mike Brearley objected. He rightly claimed that in accordance with Law Five, either captain could claim a new ball. He was overruled, something that probably would not have happened in England with a senior umpire on duty. There is, in fact, no substitute for groundwork which is why I consistently backed the idea of bringing overseas umpires over to England to take part in the County Championship. Tom Brooks (Australia), Douglas Sang Hue (West Indies) and Fred Goodall (New Zealand) all told me that they benefited from a spell on the county circuit, doing the job on a day-to-day basis alongside one of the English umpires, and I would like to see this scheme revived.

One distinguished visitor with whom I worked was Shakoor Rana, from Pakistan. He came over to this country in 1981 and we stood together at Essex early in the summer. We had two matches at Ilford, and both were interesting for different reasons. Essex won the first by ninety-five runs on a turning pitch and Middlesex had their seven bonus points deducted for including an unregistered player in their eleven.

Sussex provided the opposition in the second half of the week and they completed a very impressive victory by an innings and twenty-one runs. Sussex

scored 436 for four before declaring to take full advantage of the conditions, which still helped the slower bowlers, and their spinners made the most of them. The Sussex captain, John Barclay, obviously featured prominently with his off-spinners and as I watched from square leg I could see that he and Shakoor Rana were having a lot to say to each other.

I did not take much notice since it was not really my business, but suddenly Shakoor Rana came marching over to me. 'What is the difficulty?' I asked. 'I am giving the bowler a final warning. He is running on the pitch,' he said. I made a note of this and my colleague returned to the bowler's end, where Barclay was inspecting the pitch with a puzzled expression on his face. Shakoor Rana returned for another word. 'I want you to come,' he insisted. 'The bowler does not agree with me and he is the captain.' Really the opinion of the bowler or the square leg umpire does not matter, but I tried to lend a helping hand.

'I am not running on the pitch,' said Barclay. 'Have a look and see if you can find any marks.'

All the players were intently studying the disputed area, so I said: 'You've had an official warning, let's get on with the game.' This is just what we did and happily Shakoor Rana appeared satisfied with Barclay's bowling for the rest of the innings.

The well-upholstered figure of Indian umpire Swarup Krishnan officiating in Calcutta during a Test Match between India and England.

He was definitely a cool customer. On the Saturday night when we parted company, I said: 'I'll see you tomorrow for the Sunday League game. I shall be here for 11.30, but you do not have to arrive before 12.00.' Hew smiled politely and replied: 'I shall be here for 1.45.' To me that was cutting things very fine for a 2.00 start, but on the dot he strolled across the field wearing his big green Pakistan blazer as if he had all the time in the world.

After the Sussex fixture he picked up my white cap and said: 'You won't mind if I take a souvenir, will you?' I sighed – another one gone.

From my own first-hand experience, I am convinced that this is the best way to raise worldwide standards.

There is no doubt that I have learned a lot on my travels and also made many good friends. One of the biggest in all senses of the word is the popular Indian Swarup Krishnan Reu, who officiated in the first Test between England and India in Bombay in 1984, when some criticisms were registered. He did not reappear in that series. I partnered him during the Asian Cup competition in Sharjah in 1984 and formed a pretty high opinion of his ability.

He is, of course, as great a character as he is a man. He chews betel nut and spits frequently, rather like one of those cowboys in the old western films. I gather that betel nut is similar to tobacco when you chew it, but I decided not to risk putting that to the test when he offered me some.

As we walked out together for the first time in the game between Pakistan and Sri Lanka, he said: 'I have often prayed that one day I would be umpiring with you. Now my prayers have been answered.' I was pretty flattered, but had to tell him he would cause a few problems for bowlers in England, especially the left-arm spinners trying to go round the wicket. 'I know that, Dickie,' he said with a huge grin. 'Your Derek Underwood could never bowl from my end, he could not get around me. Phil Edmonds has had difficulties. He says I upset his rhythm.'

One idea I am very much against is the introduction of a third umpire. This has been suggested on two counts. A fanciful notion is to have an umpire in the pavilion watching television – presumably this relates only to Test cricket – so that the men at the centre of the action can seek his aid when faced with a tricky decision. It is also thought in some quarters that umpires get tired and that a rota would help, two men on and one off, allowing each to take a rest in turn.

For neither reason does a third official get any support form me. Just think of the long delay while the umpire on the field consulted his colleague in the dressing room, with everyone in suspense. As for the rota, I like to be involved in a Test match from start to finish, so I would not be able to relax during my so-called rest period. Also, having a third man could lead to inconsistency.

As a matter of record, the sixty-overs-a-side one-day games are the real stamina tests, for the average Test match day is well below 120 overs in duration.

Electronic Aids

SCIENCE IS A WONDERFUL THING and many clever inventions have improved the quality of life in various ways. Our grandparents would, for example, be astounded at things like automatic washers which take so much of the drudgery out of housework. By and large, however, these devices are labour saving, sparing the muscles rather than the mind, and I know I speak for all umpires when I say that electronic gadgets would neither improve cricket nor guarantee that we would get correct decisions all the time.

To bring them in must take something away from the umpire's authority, which is so important. The players cannot have a man-to-man understanding with a machine. Already I suspect that television, with its constant playbacks, has changed a lot of attitudes – and not for the better.

When I was a batsman with Yorkshire and Leicestershire there were times when I realized I had been on the receiving end of a bad mistake, but I simply got on with the job and never considered complaining. Indeed, most captains in the past handed out a dressing down if they found any of their team querying umpires' rulings in public and a lot frowned on moaning about it in private.

That is how it should be, for the final decision is based on a lot of things. I cannot, for example, see how any electronic device can help in assessing whether a batsman is lbw. The umpire has to weigh up several factors in his mind and then use his hard-earned knowledge to decide the probable outcome of a particular delivery.

From where did the bowler let the ball go? Was he wide on the crease or close to the stumps? How much has the ball been swinging through the air or moving off the pitch? How much bounce is there? Did the batsman get a faint touch to the ball?

It is said that the camera cannot lie. Fair enough, but it can certainly mislead, and I have talked to experts in the field of television who query its value as a final arbiter. In any case, not even the most sophisticated computer can cope

*The tourists appeal for a catch at the wicket off Geoff Boycott, who was given not out
by umpire Arthur Fagg. England v. West Indies, Edgbaston, 1973.*

with changing conditions. The new ball swings much more than one that has been hit about for a while and some balls keep their shine longer than others. Some bowlers get more movement with the seam, others gain greater purchase from it for their spin.

The good umpire appreciates all this, knows the players taking part and is thus able to make subtle allowances. A ball that on television might appear to be going on to hit the stumps could lead to a 'not out' decision for a lot of reasons.

Equally, unless the batsman and the ball are wired up to some complicated electronic eye system, catches at the wicket from those slight edges cannot be settled with utter certainty. Anyone looking back to the arguments over the West Indies *v*. England Test at Edgbaston in 1973 must agree. The tourists were convinced that Geoff Boycott should have been given out when they appealed for a catch behind by Deryck Murray off the bowling of Keith Boyce. From square leg I was not in a position to pass an opinion. All I do know is that Arthur Fagg ruled in Boycott's favour and never wavered.

The television people showed the incident time and again I have seen it with the recorder slowed down so that the ball is barely moving, but it is impossible to be positive. Arthur relied on his experience as both umpire and top-class batsman and that ought to be good enough.

With these two methods of dismissal in mind, we also have to work out just where the camera might be situated. To be of any serious value all pictures must be taken from immediately over the stumps at the bowler's end and this really is impossible. First of all, the umpire is stationed there – and I assume that no one suggests that the human element be done away with altogether. After all, no-balls, intimidation and other aspects of play would have to be dealt with in the traditional manner.

Then there is the bowler. He had to be able to make a stop or take a catch off his own bowling and the umpire can get out of the way. The camera is somewhat less agile. Even if some way of siting this important piece of equipment were to be found, there is the constant danger of someone running across the lens at the vital moment, thus blocking any meaningful picture. Here again, the umpire can adjust quickly to changing circumstance.

It is just arguable that run-outs could be settled by artificial means, although again the players can hardly be expected to keep clear of the line of vision, so it would still be necessary to have the umpire involved at all times.

The scientist, Sir Bernard Lovell is all for experiments with electronic aids and I respect his expertise in his own complicated field, but I believe that if I met him to discuss the technical problems I would open his eyes, for I suspect he is unaware of some of the cricketing objections.

There are obvious financial questions, too. I shudder to think how much it would cost to equip every county ground in the country and I feel strongly that if you were to have electronic gadgets in one game you would have to have them in all matches. Anything else has to be unfair. Counties such as Yorkshire and Essex, who regularly take the first-class game to a number of centres, would have huge problems, especially if a lot of equipment were to be required.

I also wonder how often you would have to stop play to check out the findings of the camera, for constant hold-ups are not likely to find favour with the spectators or the players. Let's suppose that in a vital fixture with one or two runs needed for a side to win and the last pair together, a big appeal went up for lbw with the ball being deflected off the pad to third man.

It would be natural for the batsmen to start running and, under the present system, they would know at once whether the striker had been given out. If, however, the umpire had to call in an outside agency, there would have to be a pause. The batsmen would be in a quandary and their concentration broken. Perhaps the umpire could say: 'Keep running, lads, and I'll let you know in a minute whether they count.' It is all too confusing to make much sense, and when the whole business is considered calmly, the logical course is to press on as we are now.

There are not all that many mistakes. Not enough anyway to justify the expense and complications that science might bring to our straightforward summer sport. In fact, a case can be made for removing what few aids are used already. The showing of incidents on a big screen, as has happened in Australia, is a step towards trouble. If it looks as though a home player has, let us say, been unlucky, it is probable that his supporters will register a protest and I am afraid that not everybody does so in a reasonable manner. There is the likelihood of spectators coming on to the field and there is too much of that already.

It cannot be stressed too often or too strongly that umpires are honest men. The word neutral has been used in the previous chapter, and another accurate description is impartial – as impartial as any piece of machinery and just as reliable.

I am, however, prepared to accept that light meters have been a success, although the original assessment of the light is made with the human eye. I have seen some wonderful contests in conditions which a computer would have ruled as unfit.

The famous Gillette Cup semi-final between Lancashire and Gloucestershire at Old Trafford is a fine example. We finished at 9.00 pm when it was, quite simply, dark. The moon beamed bright and clear from the night sky, as did the lights on Warwick Road Station, but nobody really cared.

Arthur Jepson and I had a chat after we had lost a fair bit of time to rain. We realized the danger of not completing the tie with so much to make up and thought, in fairness to both sides in such an important match, that an early agreement had to be reached.

The evening turned out to be sunlit and, with the weather set fair, we asked Lancashire captain Jack Bond, who was batting with Jack Simmons, what he wanted to do. Lancashire had slipped a long way behind the required rate and Bond said: 'We can't win, so we might as well carry on to the end. There is no point in coming back tomorrow and, in any case, if we come off now this lot will lynch us.' He pointed to the spectators crammed into every nook and cranny of the ground with the gates firmly locked since early morning.

He was right, although in the end a light meter would not have agreed. It soon became dusk and Arthur pointed out: 'Ah well, it's not so bad, the moon is out.' The rest is part of cricket folk lore, for not only did we get through to a finish, but Lancashire won with some of the most spectacular hitting there has been in any county game.

In doing so, they underlined an interesting point which few appreciate. It is often more difficult for the fielding side in really bad light, for once the ball is hit no one is really sure where it has gone and runs are cheap. It might be in the air, but the chances of a catch are remote and the bowler has really to hit the stumps to gain a wicket.

A similar situation arose in the Benson and Hedges Cup Final at Lord's in 1983, although this time, in the evening gloom, the side batting second, Essex, lost to Middlesex. The respective captains, Keith Fletcher and Mike Gatting, agreed before the start to continue more or less whatever happened and there were no complaints. Complications had arisen when light morning rain held up the start by fifty minutes, but Essex chose to field first well aware of what might happen.

Despite the light, young John Carr, son of Donald, the secretary of the Test and County Cricket Board, held a very good running catch at deep mid-on to dispose of Stuart Turner. It was a fine effort, for he had just come on as substitute for Neil Williams and had hardly had time to adjust to the conditions. Actually this was an instance in which the batsmen did seem to be the more handicapped, for Essex lost their last four wickets for seven runs, to be beaten by four when apparently set for victory.

These one-day games have to be settled. The public expect a result and have paid good money to see one. There is nothing more frustrating than having to leave things in the balance.

Barrie Meyer and I were the first umpires to use light meters. They were introduced in 1978 largely as a result of an unfortunate incident at Trent Bridge in the second Test of that year, with New Zealand being beaten by an innings and 119 runs. The umpires at Nottingham were David Constant and Tom Spencer. They had a dilemma on the Saturday morning with a light drizzle falling from grey skies. They knew they might have to come off because of the light, but they were also aware that the public were demanding action. In trying to do their best for all concerned they were in an impossible position.

They elected to play, but after only two balls had been delivered they realized that the conditions were not after all satisfactory so they brought the players off. Under the regulations, the pitch could not be covered until play had been abandoned for the day and the consequence was that New Zealand eventually had to bat on a wet surface some four hours later. They were dismissed for 120 and understandably felt badly done by as they followed on.

Mike Brearley and Ian Botham watch as Bird and Barry Meyer
deal with an intrusive spectator – England v. New Zealand, Lord's, 1978.

While the pros and cons were being debated, a photographer casually observed that according to his light meter the conditions when play was proceeding in the afternoon had been exactly the same as when they started in the morning. For once, this scientific fact had a real value.

It planted the seeds of an important idea in some official minds. Barrie and I were given a brief lecture on how the meters worked by Patrick Eagar, the well-known photographer who specializes so brilliantly in cricket, and were told to use them in the third Test at Lord's. No one, I imagine, will be in the least surprised to learn that the light remained perfect throughout and we never had to rely on our pocket-sized assistants.

I am impressed by the possibilities of artificial turf, which has been tested in some indoor cricket centres and also installed on a number of county squares.

No doubt Championship matches have to be played on normal pitches, but I have listened carefully to the opinions of such as Tom Graveney, that most stylish of English batsmen, and Gary Sobers and to a degree support their view that man-made materials can provide an acceptable playing surface.

Graveny has been associated with a company manufacturing 'carpets' and argues forcefully that they could be used for limited-overs competitions. Artificial pitches might, for one thing, reduce the importance of the toss, which in some games is virtually decisive. They are less affected by weather and would thus allow early starts, reducing the likelihood of bad light exerting an influence over the outcome.

These points are worthwhile in themselves, but there is another application for this development. Boys learning the art of batsmanship need to have confidence in the pitch upon which they practise their strokes, but the preparation of a totally reliable strip requires hours of patient and regular work. Inevitably there are shortcomings in many pitches and youngsters find the ball leaping at their untutored heads. The outcome is a loss of interest if nothing worse. Schools and junior organisations may be able to install these man-made pitches to good purpose, helping future generations of cricketers in the most positive way.

CHAPTER

With the Ladies

WOMEN'S SPORT, such as tennis and golf, is usually regarded as something of a joke by men, whose opinions are based on the comparisons between the differences in sheer power which make it impossible for the two sexes to compete on anything approaching equal terms. I never join those who sneer at the ladies, however. From first-hand knowledge I can say with every confidence that they play a pretty mean game of cricket, and some are very good.

They do lack the strength of their male counterparts and cannot achieve the same pace with their bowling, but in all other departments those at the top have tremendous ability.

I came into contact with women's cricket for the first time when I umpired a three-a-side indoor competition. The girls from the Lady Mabel College of Physical Education at Wentworth made me their official coach and I soon came to appreciate that they were serious about improving their standards.

It was, however, the very long arm of coincidence which brought about my association with the women's World Cup in New Zealand during January and February in 1982.

Michael Parkinson, an erstwhile Barnsley batsman turned cricket writer and chat show host.

As a young lad I opened the innings for Barnsley youth team and the Yorkshire League side with a likely lad called Michael Parkinson, who proved more than useful at club level before branching out into journalism and television. We both talked about representing Yorkshire and I am sure that despite all his success and fame he still nurses a slight regret at not getting farther in cricket.

We played youth matches all over the county and, at that time, the driving force and enthusiasm behind the Wakefield team was a lady called Mary Britto.

She impressed me with her expertise and feeling for cricket and I often wondered what had happened to her after we went our separate ways. The answer to that question came out of the blue one cold winter morning in 1981 when cricket was no more than a thought and icicles decorated most of the country.

A letter arrived from Mary, who had become chairman of the New Zealand Women's Cricket Council, asking me to umpire in the World Cup competition they were promoting. I do not like snow and frost so I needed no second invitation and replied at once to say I would be delighted to take part, approaching the project with an open mind. I looked forward to seeing just how good the best women cricketers in the world had become.

I spent six weeks in New Zealand altogether, including a two-week holiday with some good friends from the Leeds area. This was not a new venture, for the first women's World Cup had been staged in England in 1973, when a businessman named Jack Hayward provided the financial backing and seven teams took part – England, Australia, Jamaica, New Zealand, Trinidad and Tobago, Young England and an International Eleven. A series of sixty-overs-per-side matches produced an England triumph, for they beat Australia in the final by ninety-two runs.

The expenses were very high and the women rightly feel they are the poor relations of world cricket. Sponsorship, which the men attract so readily, is scarce largely because the publicity and, therefore, the attendances are limited. The newspapers and television give precious little coverage, so commercial companies putting money into the women's World Cup do not get a lot back.

The girls have to pay the bulk of their own costs. Massive fund raising is needed to get the World Cup off the ground. A lack of ready money restricted the scope, but a second World Cup took place in India in 1978, although only four countries were represented.

England, Australia, India and New Zealand kept the flag flying, with the Australians taking the trophy after reversing the result from that first final. When New Zealand's turn came around, they formed a World Cup committee and issued invitations to England, Australia, West Indies, Holland and India. Holland and the West Indies withdrew, forcing a rearrangement of the original programme to bring in an International Eleven. Three preliminary rounds culminated in the final at Christchurch.

I umpired several ties, including the final, which gives me a unique record of officiating in both the men's and women's World Cup finals. New Zealander Fred Goodall also took part, along with a number of women umpires, who all operated very efficiently, and the whole thing went off extremely well. Australia emerged as winners. England scored 151 for five in their sixty overs in the final and Australia had three wickets in hand when they passed that total with one over to spare.

The quality of the cricket was high. The girls put on a show of neat stroke-play, while the fielding gave nothing away, and many of them looked good enough to hold down a place in a reasonable league team in England.

Sharon Tredrea, the Australian captain from Victoria, was the quickest bowler on view and I can think of one or two batsmen who would have been wary against her on a pacy pitch. She is a strongly built girl with a good action. I put her at about the pace of Hampshire's Tim Tremlett, a seam bowler with a good record and a sound reputation on the county circuit. I mentioned that I had been impressed with her ability to work up genuine speed and she said: 'If you had seen me three years ago, you would certainly have got a shock. I was a lot quicker then.'

I travelled with the England team to New Plymouth, which boasts one of the most picturesque grounds in the world, flying in from Auckland. The airbus in which we were to fly looked a bit on the ancient side with its four propellers, so when a delay was announced we all had an anxious moment. In fact, the captain could not get it started. Out we all got to give him a good push which did

Australia's Sharon Tredrea bowling against England at Edgbaston in 1976.

the trick, and I bet a lot of photo-graphers regret not being about to grab a shot of me and the girls putting our shoulders to the rear end of an aeroplane. We had landed again before we got our breath and confidence back.

Jan Brittin stood out among the English girls. The Surrey all-rounder is a superb athlete and has represented the English schools at athletics. She picked up 391 runs in the competition, employing a wide range of quality strokes, and had the highest aggregate, so I accept without question the fact that she scores steadily when playing against men.

Another good cricketer is Jan Southgate, who came from Sussex. She did not play in the early matches in New Zealand, but, as I watched her in the nets, I formed the opinion that the selectors ought to think again. I had a quiet word on her behalf and they must have taken notice, for she was chosen for the next match, did well, and went on to become one of the most successful English batsmen. That, by the way, is not a slip of the pen. The girls themselves refer to 'batsmen' rather than 'batswomen', acknowledging that it sounds more natural.

Australia, in retaining the trophy, proved the better side and confirmed their superiority when England toured their country in the 1984–5 winter.

I had the pleasure of meeting the New Zealand Prime Minister, Sir Robert Muldoon at a civic reception and received VIP treatment all the way. New Zealand Airways sponsored my trip and their wonderful hospitality led to an embarrassing moment on the way home.

The captain of the aeroplane turned out to be a cricket fanatic and when he discovered that I was among the passengers he invited me to the flight deck, where I spent a fascinating couple of hours learning something about how it operated and also talking about the game. As I returned to my seat, he instructed the steward: 'Give Dickie a couple of bottles of our best wine with my compliments.' I put these carefully into the bag with my cabin luggage, but, as we changed planes in Los Angeles, I dropped it and they broke. There was wine all over the place. It soaked all the things in my bag and to this day the souvenir programmes are crinkled and blotchy. They smell quite nice, though!

Competing so seriously, the women need the same sort of body protection as the men – and a bit more besides. I umpired a game between England and Australia, who had in their side Denise Alderman, from Western Australia. She is the sister of Terry Alderman, the Australian seamer who had a season in England with Kent. While she was batting, the England bowler, wicket-keeper and close fielders appealed convincingly for a catch behind. I heard some contact, but, not certain the ball had touched the bat, I gave 'not out'.

When Denise got down to my end, she said: 'That was a neat decision. The ball hit my chest protector which is metal.'

I discovered another advantage to having the ladies around when I injured myself. Whenever I shower I put on my floppy sandals to avoid slipping. Once in New Zealand I forget them and, sure enough, fell heavily, badly bruising my right elbow. Happily the place was full of budding Florence Nightingales and I could not help but make a speedy recovery, although I have to admit that I still get a twinge now and again.

The visit to New Zealand gave me the chance to umpire in the Shell Shield Final between Wellington and Canterbury at Lancaster Park, a ground which also stages football matches. They have an area behind the bowler's arm at one end which is the equivalent of the Hill at Sydney, albeit on a smaller scale.

When the fans have had a few beers they get very lively, and during the final they were throwing cans on to the field and reflecting the sun into the batsmen's eyes – a little trick they enjoyed performing irrespective of the way the game was going.

Eventually one of the batting team asked me if I would try and do something about the distractions and particularly the blinding lights. I set off straight away, keen to restore order, but as I marched to deal with the offenders I noticed that the fielders were laughing and enjoying a private joke. 'All right, gentlemen, what's so funny?' I demanded. 'You'll find out if you get caught up in that lot,' one replied, pointing to the sprawling mob stretched out in the sunshine. 'What we really want is a lion tamer,' added another.

The shouting and jeering grew as I approached the boundary. I held up my arms and at once gained the attention of a lot of people. 'Do you mind if we continue with our match?' I asked, trying to put on a stern expression. That provoked a roar of laughter and in a few minutes I had made a lot of friends in that area. 'Right,' I said, 'I'll have another chat with you later, but I don't want any more interruptions until the final is over.' They cheered me all the way back to the middle and behaved themselves for the rest of the day, much to the astonishment of the players.

Wellington is called the 'Windy City' and when we were there it lived up to its name with a vengeance. Even the weighted bails refused to stay on the stumps and when England's Sue Goatman and Barbara Bevege, of New Zealand, tossed up, the coin was blown almost to the boundary. The bowlers could hardly stand up with the wind whistling straight down the pitch. From one end they were pushed along so that they found difficulty in stopping to deliver the ball, while at the other they could hardly reach the stumps. All concerned battled with commendable spirit, though, and no one complained.

In Auckland I was honoured by an invitation from the mayor and council of Birkenhead to visit the city and I took along a booklet on Barnsley to give them. That, I suppose, made me an ambassador for my home town, so the women's World Cup proved a very interesting experience in many ways.

Caribbean Carnival

World beater –
Clive Lloyd lifts the
trophy after the West
Indies beat Australia
in the first World Cup
Final at Lord's in 1975.
Uniquely, Bird stood
in each of the first three
finals.

O NE-DAY CRICKET is not everybody's cup of tea. The traditionalists will always prefer the County Championship or Test matches and I can understand their thinking. Most players share the view that the game is at its best when there is time to bring out all the subtleties of the contest between bat and ball. To many cricket lovers a maiden over by that great Australian paceman Ray Lindwall to England's batting hero Len Hutton justified the expense and travelling time for a day at the cricket and there have been many marvellous passages of play which have produced few runs and little breathless excitement. The slow build-up is part of cricket's fascination.

Time, however, moves on and a generation of spectators has grown up with different values. To them cricket is the hurly-burly of the limited-overs competitions which usually contain high drama and instant results. These can hinge on one single act, and in close finishes the tension is readily apparent on the field and in the crowd. There is no doubt that this form of county cricket has attracted spectators who would otherwise never have seen the game at that level and brought in thousands of pounds to the relief of the hard-pressed senior clubs. Indeed, without the cash from the John Player League, the Benson and Hedges Cup and the Nat-West Trophy the first-class game may not have survived.

The one-day internationals proved very popular and the public have flocked to see the best performers in the world squeezing their skills into the frame-work of a format that guarantees a 'sudden-death' conclusion. There have been three World Cup finals and I have had the great honour of officiating in them all – the only man to do so. I stood with Tommy Spencer in 1975, when the West Indies beat Australia, while Barrie Meyer was my partner in the second in 1979, when the West Indies completed a double by overcoming England, and again in 1983, India's year.

The tremendous sense of occasion is heightened by a visit to Buckingham Palace before the finals. I sometimes find it hard to believe that I have now met

Her Majesty the Queen seven times. Then there is the drive down the Mall in the team buses with the national flags flying, which is also something very special.

Whatever the purists may say, I regard the 1975 final as just about the best game of cricket I have seen, for the quality of play throughout remained incredibly high and every session contained a dramatic turn of fortune which left the packed Lord's ground buzzing.

The slow pitch allowed very little movement, but the bounce occasionally trapped the unwary into a false stroke. The action began when the West Indies, who were put in, lost their first wicket in the most remarkable and unlucky way. Roy Fredericks, a dashing stroke-maker, displayed his lightning reflexes to swing a short ball from Dennis Lillee high into the mass of spectators, who were busy celebrating this spectacular hit when it became clear that the batsman had lost his balance and knocked off a bail.

Perhaps the West Indies were unnerved by this accident of fate, for their innings lost its momentum and they struggled along against some accurate bowling. There were a few question marks about their temperament, which seem silly now, but when they lost their third wicket at fifty, Rohan Kanhai said to me sadly; 'We are in a very bad position. It will be hard to win this one from here.'

Had I said anything I would have agreed, but Clive Lord was approaching the wicket in that rather apologetic dawdle of his. He appeared tired and weighed down by the set-backs, but he was on his way to produce as fine an innings as any in his career.

I cannot recollect even the slightest hint of an error as he swept along to 102, making those runs from only eighty-two balls. Jeff Thomson, his reputation well established, had his familiar trouble with his front foot and got called a number of times for over-stepping, but he worked up a very hostile pace. The shots came in a rush which captured the imagination of the crowd, and by the time he was out, caught down the leg side of the persistent Gary Gilmour, Lloyd had put the West Indies back on course.

They closed at 291 for eight, which left Australia to score at almost five an over to win. They made a very brave attempt. Alan Turner and Ian Chappell pushed the singles and hammered the bad balls – some of which were not all that bad – and stayed in sight of the target.

In fact, I am sure that the Australians would have got those runs had they not panicked and thrown away three key wickets with the issue in the balance. Foolish running brought run-outs at a crucial time and, not learning the lesson, they sacrificed more men in the same way later in the innings.

It is often forgotten that Viv Richards was the man responsible for all three of those early run-outs, so perhaps there is some excuse for the Australians.

Viv Richards batting at Lord's during the 1979 World Cup Final,
when West Indies beat England to retain the trophy.

Richards is like a cat in the field. To all appearances drowsily taking in the sun-shine, he reacts instinctively to the possibility of despatching a careless batsman. In this case, Richards threw down the stumps from midwicket to run out Turner, ending the second-wicket stand of fifty-six. Again from midwicket he accounted for Greg Chappell after the brothers had put on thirty-four with growing assur-ance. Finally, his bullet-like return to Lloyd left Ian Chappell out of his ground.

Australia, their composure shattered, lost a ninth wicket at 233, at which stage they required another fifty-nine for victory. Dennis Lillee is a well-organized customer to be coming in at number eleven and he had not given up the ghost by any means. As he reached my end he muttered: 'We can still win this.' He might well have been talking to himself and I did not want to disturb his concentration, so I kept quiet, but as the required rate stood at four an over I regarded the task as bordering on the impossible.

The West Indies opted to give the last pair singles to save the boundaries, and the runs came steadily. I began to change my mind. In these one-off situations things can easily get out of hand because players are keyed up and one or two West Indians began casting anxious glances at the scoreboard as it ticked remorselessly along.

To supplement the diet of ones and twos, Australia had to hit some boundaries. Both Lillee and Thomson took the odd chance by aiming a big swing. From one of them, Lillee hoisted a catch, but in all the hubbub no one heard Tom call 'No-ball'. Spectators surged on to the field and smothered play in their thousands. You could hardly see a blade of grass.

Somebody hit me a heavy blow on the side of the head as they snatched my white cap. I felt dizzy for a moment, but then noticed that Thomson and Lillee were still running between the wickets, pushing their way through the dancing West Indian supporters. 'Keep going,' Lillee shouted as they passed close to me. 'One of this lot could have the ball in his pocket,' warned Thomson, but they panted along. 'How many have we got?' asked Thomson. 'Twelve,' came the confident reply.

Fortunately, the police had handled the crowd throughout with a lot of friendly good humour, creating an excellent relationship which probably saved the day. Despite all the noise and good cheer, the spectators gradually realized that we wanted to get on with the game and the playing area was cleared. The batsmen pulled to a breathless halt. 'How many have you run altogether then?' I enquired of Lillee. 'Seventeen, mate,' he said with a broad grin. 'Well, that's bad luck, because you are only getting four,' I informed him. Roy Fredericks had hurled the ball at the stumps in an attempt to claim a run-out off the no-ball, keeping his cool in a tight situation. He missed and the ball disappeared among the onrushing hordes, so, according to the laws, we awarded four runs and called the ball 'dead'.

The hold-up did not help the Australians and Thomson subsequently became the fifth run-out victim of the innings to leave the West Indies winners by seventeen runs. Nothing in the world could have stopped the second cavalry charge by their fans, who wanted a reminder of the great day. They meant no harm, but they virtually stripped Keith Boyce, taking even his boots, while Thomson lost his bat and had his pads ripped off. He was one of the last players to leave the field after finishing on the floor as he dived in a desperate attempt to reach the crease.

The stumps, of course, went, although this did not matter much because during the tea interval we had the good set removed and some old ones brought out to take their place. There is no way you can protect things. If you let the West Indians have their momentoes they do not do any real damage, but if you try to hang on to them a tug of war develops and you can get hurt. Nowadays before a series with the West Indies starts I have a box of caps sent from Luton in the sure knowledge that I am going to lose one or two.

This was another match to finish in poor light and there were some thoughts given to reducing the number of overs. Ian Chappell felt it had been a very long day and said that the players were very tired. Actually they had had it a bit easier than the umpires. We were on duty from 8.30 in the morning until the finish at around 9.00 pm. Both Tom and I felt weary.

Tom did well to get through. He took a big blow on the shin from a hard drive by Australian Doug Walters and his leg bled heavily. We had a brief discussion about what to do and he said: 'I'll manage. The game has to go on.' The doctor patched him up a bit, but he had a lot of pain towards the end.

We agreed, though, that we would not have missed the final for all the world and, having come through successfully, with no complaints from either side, I felt ready to tackle anything.

By comparison, the 1979 final proceeded along fairly ordinary lines. The result was rarely in doubt as the West Indies beat England by ninety-two runs. By now everybody had become more accustomed to the glamour of the World Cup. Even so, England's presence at Lord's grabbed the attention of the nation's cricket watchers and there was plenty to discuss.

England's decision to leave Essex seam bowler John Lever out of their squad was reckoned to be a mistake and, whatever the merits of the arguments, captain Mike Brearley had to 'find' twelve overs from his less practised and recognized bowlers. This became an important factor as the West Indies made 286 for nine from their sixty overs. With this sort of total at their backs, the battery of quick bowlers – Andy Roberts, Michael Holding, Colin Croft and Joel Garner – had to fancy their chances and I felt England were in trouble before the end of the West Indies innings.

Geoff Boycott got through six overs for thirty-eight, which was not bad, but he had suffered back trouble for a long time and could not be expected to do much more. Graham Gooch bowled four overs for twenty-seven and Wayne

Larkin two for twenty-one – so that eighty-six runs came from this weakness. Richards and Collis King, who made up the extra overs in the West Indian attack, allowed only forty-eight runs from thirteen.

Richards had no challengers as Man of the Match, for he effectively turned the game after England had done very well to claim four wickets for ninety-nine. England, in breaking through so decisively, had put the West Indies in a similar situation to four years previously. Now Richards took over Lloyd's role. So much depended upon him and he scratched about for his first fifty, playing and missing a few times at the moving ball. Had he got an edge England could easily have become champions and they stayed in the hunt for quite a while.

Gradually Richards came to terms with his timing, putting on 139 in only twenty-one overs with King to swing the initiative away from Brearley and his team. I thought King's innings of eighty-nine was magnificent. Definitely the West Indies were in trouble when he went to the wicket.

*Viv Richards loses his
wicket during India's
triumph in the 1983
final, caught by Kapil
Dev off Madan Lal.*

The England opening stand between Brearley and Boycott became the topic for fierce debate. This pair put on 129, but used up too many overs. They had to contend with a stream of fast bowling and everyone in the home camp must have been happy with a tea score of seventy-nine without loss from twenty-five overs. Lloyd showed no concern over the situation, shrugging off the failure of his bowlers to make an impact. 'I thought they would have opened with Gooch,' he said. 'They are scoring only at three an over and that's not bad for us.'

Brearley claimed that England were in a good position at tea, but he and Boycott pushed Richards for a lot of singles when they ought to have been finding the boundary. Boycott, incidentally, wore a protective helmet for the first time and I wondered if this inhibited him. England approached the last phase of their innings needing to score at eight an over, which was impossible against Garner. As Brearley observed: 'He is the only man I know who bowls out of the trees at the Nursery End. When he pitches the ball well it is impossible to see it.' Big Bird took five of the last seven wickets, firing fast and straight into the base of the stumps. He offered nothing at all that might have been hit and survival is not enough in these one-day games.

During the 1983 tournament another former Yorkshire batsman, Barrie Leadbeater, joined me on the list and we umpired together in the group game between New Zealand and Pakistan at Edgbaston. Little Zimbabwe, finding their feet among the big boys of world cricket, had their moment of glory when they beat the mighty Australians at Trent Bridge, scoring 239 to 226. While my pals from 'down under' did not think much about that result it did a lot of good for the game as a whole, besides giving a hint that there are very fine cricketers in unexpected parts of the globe.

Zimbabwe's Duncan Fletcher hits out at Australia's Jeff Thomson during the 1983 World Cup.

Far less pleasant were some of the scenes which marred India's semi-final triumph over England at Old Trafford. They won easily by six wickets, operating throughout with style, and it became obvious that their supporters were all set to invade the field when the winning hit arrived.

The England fielders made their own preparations for hurried departures to the safety of the pavilion and umpire Don Oslear had the longest dash to make. He ran into trouble and needed a stump to defend himself. I appreciate that there is a danger when you are surrounded, but it is easy to over-react and I believe Don would have been wiser to adopt a more relaxed approach.

Don cares a lot about cricket and actually helped to restrain a spectator at a Sunday League game between Yorkshire and Leicestershire at Scarborough in 1983. The man came on to the ground and ran up to the stumps, where Don held him until the police took over. 'I'll do anything I can to save the game for the players and the real followers,' he said to me afterwards.

Zimbabwe's success over the Australians illustrated the glorious uncertainty of cricket and Sri Lanka's triumph by three wickets at the expense of New Zealand confirmed it. De Silva, returning the remarkable one-day figures of 12-5-11-2, demonstrated with unassuming efficiency that leg-spinners have a place in the game at all levels, provided they are good enough. New Zealand could manage only 181 at Derby and, despite a few stutters, the minnows scrambled home.

While all this was going on, India beat the West Indies at Old Trafford in a Group B match. This was the first defeat in the World Cup for the Caribbean Cavaliers, whose natural game is so suited to the requirements of the limited-overs competition, and Barrie Leadbeater brought the news that India had been very impressive.

One of the features of the performance was the solid team-work. Yashpal Sharma scored eighty-nine in a total of 262 for eight, but there were steady contributions from several others. The pattern remained much the same when the West Indies replied. Left-arm spinner Ravi Shastri, who has since advertized his claims as a world-class all-rounder, gave a glimpse of his ability with a tidy spell that earned him three wickets as India collected the qualifying points by thirty-four runs.

That at least prepared people for their victory over England at Old Trafford in the semi-final, but it hardly set the stage for what was to occur at Lord's. Odd uncertainties in a group fixture were one thing, but the final was a different matter altogether. I do not suppose that more than a handful of neutral observers thought India would do more than make up the numbers.

They seemed unlikely to stretch the West Indies when they got themselves out for only 183 on a perfect batting pitch. The West Indies bowled well, of course, but I had a lot of sympathy for the Indians, who were not doing as well as they could.

Srikkanth got them off on a high note after they had been put in, but there was too much carelessness. The brilliant Kapil Dev hardly set a good example as captain, throwing the bat like a millionaire and getting out to the gentle medium pace of Larry Gomes. As they began their reply, the West Indies must have thought that a hat-trick of Cup wins was no more than a formality and here they made a sorry error of judgement.

I quickly noticed that the Indian medium pacers were swinging the ball a bit and getting more help from the conditions than the much faster West Indians. What a pity they did not get around 240, I said to myself. Then they would have had a chance.

Gordon Greenidge gave away his wicket, padding up to be bowled by Sandhu, but the West Indies reached fifty without further alarms before Desmond Haynes barely moved his feet in driving casually at Madan Lal to be caught. Kapil Dev strolled up to me and said: 'Do you know, we will win after all. They think it is too easy. They will get themselves out if we keep the ball well up and bowl straight.' Since Clive Lloyd was joining Viv Richards I dismissed this as wishful thinking, but the turning point came at once as the West Indies suffered two blows.

Richards has so much time to play his shots that he is accused of being lazy or careless when he gets out. This can be unfair because the margin between success and failure is so slender. At Lord's in 1983, however, Richards was definitely annoyed with himself. He had no need to hurry or indulge in extravagant gestures, but still went for the hook at Madan Lal and Dev himself judged the swirling catch to perfection, running back at mid-off.

To add to the West Indian misery, Lloyd pulled a groin muscle. He remained at the crease, batting with the aid of a runner, but in his position I would have retired. The option of coming back later remained and the presence of the runner unsettled the side. Richards shared my view of the situation, but it is easy to analyze things with the benefit of hindsight. Lloyd had to make up his mind on the spot. He did not last long and here, too, his injury probably played a part in his dismissal, for he drove Roger Binny to Dev, still coolly supervising events from mid-off. I am convinced that a fully fit Lloyd would have hit the ball a lot harder and noticed that he winced visibly as he tried to get to the pitch of the ball.

The West Indies literally limped into tea at seventy-six for five from twenty-five overs and from that point on they managed just one solitary boundary – a hook for six by Jeff Dujon. This underlines how hard the cricket became, although I am not sure that the West Indies were right to abandon their more normal attacking style. Dev turned the screw tighter and tighter. He had no room for error, but never lost his sense of purpose. Several times he said to me: 'We've got them now', possibly seeking to reassure himself.

The drama built up as the West Indies died the slow death, strangled by the Indians and their own uncertainty. It fell to me to give the final decision, which presented no difficulty since Michael Holding got into a position which left him plumb lbw to Man of the Match Mohinder Amarnath.

As I lifted the finger that pushed the champions' crown from the West Indian head, I said: 'That's out and thank you for a wonderful game, gentlemen.' Amarnath, one of the quietest figures you could ever meet, reacted like lightning to snatch one of the stumps and we all raced for the dressing room.

Within seconds the whole of the playing area had disappeared under the swarm of spectators and the new kings were confirmed.

Since then the authorities at Lord's have introduced a major improvement. They erected a temporary miniature stand in front of the Tavern Bar for the 1984 Nat West Trophy final between Middlesex and Kent. Heavy drinking has been responsible for a lot of disturbances down the years and this move cut out a lot of it. There was no trouble and the match went along very smoothly.

That's out! Bird lifts the finger, Michael Holding is lbw to Mohinder Amarnath, and India are the new World Champions, Lord's, 1983.

9

The Perfect Pitch

BILL ALLEY, THE BLUFF, BURLY AUSTRALIAN from New South Wales, became one of the best all-rounders in the world during his spell with Somerset which stretched from 1957 to 1968. A punishing left-hand batsman, he was the last player to score over 3,000 runs in an English season. He piled up 3,019 in 1961, creating a record of 2,761 for his adopted county in the process. His bowling commanded a lot of respect as well, his career tally of 768 wickets costing no more than 22.68 runs each.

Big Bill was proud of his professionalism and when he delivered a rank long hop in a match against Leicestershire at Ashby-de-la-Zouch, he pulled up with an angry expression on his face. 'I've never bowled one of those in my life,' he roared. 'There's something wrong with this pitch.' Such a complaint from a lesser man might have been dismissed out of hand, but Bill was not easy to silence and he knew he was right. Out came the groundsman to measure up and, sure enough, there had been a serious error. The stumps had been set up twenty-four yards apart instead of the regulation twenty-two. I was batting at the time for Leicestershire and I hit Bill for one or two fours – something I had never done before.

There were similarly strange goings on at Liverpool in 1979. Alan Whitehead and I were the umpires and Derbyshire the visitors to this Lancashire outpost.

The game got off to an amazing start when Barry Wood and David Lloyd opened the Lancashire innings. John Walters and Bob Wincer sprayed the new ball all over the place. Six no-balls and two wides were included in the first fifteen runs put on the board, and the bowlers began to ask questions. When we had the set-up checked we discovered that the stumps were out of alignment and they had to be put straight before play could continue. When we restarted they still bowled wides.

Another character just as determined and formidable as Bill Alley, Fred Trueman, had a particularly embarrassing experience at Harrogate. Opening the Yorkshire attack, Fred hurled three successive deliveries well wide down the leg side. 'This ruddy pitch isn't straight,' he snarled to umpire Dusty Rhodes. 'The stumps aren't in line.' He insisted that everything had to be checked, so play was held up while the groundsman brought out his chain and stretched it between the two middle stumps. The creases were also scrutinized, but everything was in perfect order. The geometry proved Fred wrong. He wiped the sweat from his brow, rubbed it into one side of the new ball, gave the other side a furious rub on his ample bottom and began the long trek back to his mark.

He could not, however, resist an aside to the non-striker who had wisely kept a straight face amidst general merriment at the fast bowler's downfall. 'I'll bet you a fiver there's summat wrong with that there chain,' said Fred.

There have, of course, been quite a few instances where the poor old groundsman has got his calculations muddled. Like umpires, this dedicated body of men have to accept that they cannot really win. They are at the mercy of the weather and the soil conditions with which they have to work and they cannot please everybody.

If a groundsman prepares a pitch with lots of runs in it, he suffers the wrath of the bowlers, but when the wickets are tumbling and the ball leaping or turning, the batsmen grumble. It is heads you win, tails I lose, for when the conditions are absolutely perfect, the players get all the praise.

Generally, the pitch is either too slow, too quick, too flat, too bouncy, too green, too bare, too wet or too dry, depending on the critic's point of view. I have done most things in cricket, but I have never prepared a pitch, although, in common with my colleagues, I compile a confidential report on them after each match.

I do not think that grass necessarily makes a good pitch, for it is used primarily to hold and bind the soil, so a fine layer of grass to protect the surface a little is enough. The main requirement for good, positive cricket is even bounce, with a bit of pace to encourage the bowlers to put all they have got into their work. In those conditions, they feel that when they beat the bat and get an edge the ball will probably carry to the slips or wicket-keeper. Thus they are encouraged to attack and try things with their fielders in close-catching positions.

Despite this, the batsmen can play their strokes. With the field close set, there is space in the outfield to collect runs and make it worthwhile to lift shots in the air, while the ball comes on to the bat to assist with timing. There is a good balance in the contest, with reward for the skilful performers and plenty to interest those watching.

There has always been a lot of argument about the covering of pitches against rain and the regulations have been altered as different views have gained the ascendancy. I feel that by covering the Test and County Cricket Board had saved a lot of matches.

Playing areas left exposed to the elements can get wet enough to hold up the action even when the weather becomes fine and dry. Additionally, since the introduction of Surrey loam, which came into regular use some years ago, wet pitches on some grounds have become very dangerous. This factor carried a lot of weight with a special sub-committee which recommended full covering.

Even so, I appreciate the arguments of those people who believe that uncovered pitches are more sporting. When pitches are protected, reasonably competent batsmen can make runs providing they avoid foolish mistakes. This means that patience can be a virtue and the entertainment value of the day's play is undermined.

On rain-affected strips, of course, the ball lifts and turns spitefully and only those batsmen possessing genuine talent and top-class techniques can hope to survive. The demands are for razor-sharp reflexes and excellent judgement. The boys are separated from the men and such as Geoff Boycott can demonstrate the arts and crafts of run-making under pressure.

Play during the First Test between England and Australia at Headingley in 1985.

It is in these circumstances that some of the greatest innings have been produced, even though they may have yielded no more than a handful of runs. One which springs instantly to mind brought Len Hutton just thirty at the Oval in August 1948. Don Bradman's invincible Australians won by an innings and 149 runs after England had decided to bat first on a ground saturated by torrential rain that delayed the start.

England's captain Norman Yardley based his decision on the theory that further rain could make matters worse for the batting side, but his men were condemned to a terrible time at the hands of Ray Lindwall, Keith Miller and Bill Johnston.

While all around him was confusion, Hutton illustrated why he was rated among the all-time greats, being last out, well caught off a genuine leg glance. England scraped together a humiliating fifty-two, but most of the spectators were enthralled by the Yorkshireman's mastery.

Controversy occurs when the pitches favour the bowlers and Headingley has been in the headlines a few times since that notable Test in 1972 when England beat Australia in three days as spinners Ray Illingworth and Derek Underwood carried nearly all before them.

George Cawthray and Keith Boyce have worked long, unsung hours to get the famous square back into shape, but it has proved a long and expensive business. Bradman, who scored 334 against England there in 1930 and 304 in 1934, rated Headingley as the best batting surface he had ever seen. I have often thought that pitches were better in the old days when chemicals were not used. Each groundsman had his own special recipe which contained things like cow

dung, water and other natural ingredients. He would flood the square and then roll it endlessly to bring about ideal conditions.

These days, squares have been relaid on some major grounds. Quite a bit of Headingley has been dug up and the soil replaced, while Old Trafford had to have special attention following Jim Laker's historic nineteen-wicket haul in 1956, when the Surrey off-spinner routed Australia. Even so, concern about the shortage of pace is being expressed at many venues and the Test and County Cricket Board have made strenuous efforts to bring about improvements.

Until some magic formula is discovered, the groundsmen will continue to labour from dawn until after dusk, doing their best and accepting the brickbats with a philosophical shrug of the shoulders.

They are a band of dedicated, warm-hearted men who care far more for the job itself than the rewards that might accrue. They are certainly not over-paid for the time they put in throughout the year. Often, after a back-breaking day, the sound of rain pattering against the bedroom window can send them rushing out into the night to make sure that the covers and the sheeting on the square are all in position and that the precious twenty-two yards on which the next game is to be played are safe and sound.

Even when the weather does not dog their footsteps and haunt their fitful dreams, there is the danger of something going wrong. Kevin Sharp, the young Yorkshire left-hander, tried his hand as a groundsman's assistant during one of his winter visits to Australia. In order to take advantage of the sun and get an even tan, he took off his watch and put it on the cab of the roller as he trundled backwards and forwards over the pitch. He had been busy for a while when he realized that the vibration had dislodged the watch which had been rolled into the ground.

Another mishap occurred at New Road, Worcester, in 1979, when Somerset were the visitors to that most beautiful of venues. The assistant groundsman rolled the starting handle of his machine into the pitch. With the heavy roller in operation, the damage was considerable. Lloyd Budd and I spoke to the captains, Norman Gifford and Brian Rose, and rang up Lord's before agreeing to move the pitch over a yard to avoid the hole.

Accidents are not the only things that cause these sort of problems. Vandalism has raised its ugly head in cricket and it is virtually impossible to protect grounds adequately when hooligans set their minds to doing something silly. After all, it does not take much to ruin a pitch – just a few holes in the right places can destroy weeks of laborious preparation.

The most sensational incident centred on the 1975 Test between England and Australia at Headingley. This was a very interesting tussle which developed along closely fought lines. Australia had to score 445 in 615 minutes to win and

Tony Greig and Ian Chappell survey the damage after vandals forced a premature end to the 1975 Headingley Test between England and Australia.

reached 220 for three at the close of play on the fourth day. Early on Tuesday morning George Cawthray discovered that his pitch had been attacked during the night. People campaigning on behalf of a man called George Davis, who, they thought, had been wrongly imprisoned, scratched some holes and poured oil into them.

They were able to go about their awful business despite the presence of a night watchman. Somehow they got into Headingley under the cloak of darkness and ironically hid under the covers which had been put in place to protect the pitch. Nothing could be done to repair the damage, and in an attempt to ensure that the Test continued the authorities considered switching to the adjoining strip intended for the Roses match on the following Saturday. This turned out to be too wet, so the game was abandoned, which was probably the best decision since the result would have been unsatisfactory whichever way it had gone once the 'stage' had been shifted. In any case, heavy rain set in around 11.00 am and continued for much of the day.

Other acts of sabotage occurred during the anti-apartheid protests in 1970 causing the proposed visit by the South Africans to be cancelled. There was no political motive behind the events which forced Yorkshire and Hampshire to improvize at Portsmouth in 1976, however. Their championship fixture was affected when the pitch was badly scarred during the Sunday night. Someone – the most logical explanation put the blame on drunken revellers, since no worthwhile clues emerged – decided it would be amusing to dig two holes around a good length at one end and, for good measure, a single hole at the other.

They used a heavy metal spike and left a considerable mark. In this instance it proved possible to transfer the remaining play to a pitch prepared for another match on the Wednesday. Umpires Lloyd Budd and Alan Whitehead, together with captains John Hampshire and Richard Gilliat, made the best of things, and Yorkshire, forced to follow on, managed to salvage a face-saving draw.

An interesting side issue in this game was that Barrie Leadbeater made his only century for Yorkshire and it came in his 208th innings for them – a remarkable statistic about a very well-organized player who scored steadily for the country. Local television covered the fixture and would have recorded this memorable occasion had they been able to get on the air. Unfortunately for Barrie the television technician did not have time to resite their scaffolding and cameras for the new pitch, so alternative programmes were put on.

Testing Time

Ｍ Y CAREER AS A TEST MATCH UMPIRE began in the lonely silence of the Leeds Rugby Club stand at Headingley as the dawn broke over the silent city on the first morning of the third game with New Zealand in 1973. The rest of that summer could not have been more crowded, nor could the Lord's pitch when we had the bomb scare a few weeks later. I got thrown in at the deep end with a vengeance and while I have enjoyed just about every minute of all the big occasions, I must admit to some anxious thoughts in that spectacular season.

It was a considerable honour to be appointed to the Test panel in only my third season on the first-class list and that promotion confirmed that I was making the right sort of progress. All the same, I regarded myself as very much the new boy as I walked up to Headingley on Thursday, 5 July.

Charlie Elliott and I were on duty, but I believe he was still sound asleep in his bed when I slipped in through the Herbert Sutcliffe gates with the stars still twinkling in the sky. I remember shivering, but I do not know whether it was because of the cold or from the sense of excitement and sheer elation at being involved in Test cricket.

I wandered about a bit, saw George Cawthray going about his normal routine and just went to sit overlooking the Rugby League field, keeping out of the way and letting my nerves settle. Had I been gifted with the ability to see into the future I would have been even more tense, but my debut went smoothly. There were no complications or hair-line decisions and I returned to the county scene well satisfied.

England won comfortably by an innings and one run and New Zealand had some difficulty in stretching their resistance into a fifth day. On a green pitch, against John Snow, Chris Old and Geoff Arnold, who could exploit the situation to the full, they were outclassed.

Ray Illingworth handled things efficiently and Geoff Boycott picked up his runs with an untroubled ease. England suited their approach to the conditions

Fleet of foot – Bird in action during his first Test,
England v. New Zealand, Headingley, 1973.

and Snow, Arnold and Old cut through the New Zealand innings by keeping a very full length. Giving an object lesson in seam bowling, they let the ball do the work, while the tourists tended to drop that bit short, allowing runs to be scored off the back foot.

This was a split tour year, with the West Indies playing three Tests in the second half of the season. I teamed up with Arthur Fagg for the second of these games at Edgbaston. The West Indies arrived in Birmingham one up after completing a very impressive victory at the Oval and they virtually made sure of not losing that advantage by scoring 327 in their first innings.

This was the first time that a visiting eleven had been composed entirely of players associated with English counties, the West Indies line-up being Roy Fredericks (Glamorgan), Ron Headley (Worcestershire), Rohan Kanhai (Warwickshire), Clive Lloyd (Lancashire), Alvin Kallicharran (Warwickshire), Gary Sobers (Nottinghamshire), Deryck Murray (Warwickshire), Bernard Julien (Kent), Keith Boyce (Essex), Vanburn Holder (Worcestershire) and Lance Gibbs (Warwickshire).

As far as the men from the Caribbean were concerned the days were over when England could gain a slight edge through being more familiar with the conditions. They were part and parcel of the English scene, more widely experienced, in fact, than their opponents.

England's reply was solid enough, with Boycott and Dennis Amiss battling resolutely, but we had to deal with an explosion of bad temper from Kanhai. He and the rest of the West Indians were convinced that Boycott had edged a catch to Murray, the wicket-keeper, off the bowling of Boyce. Arthur decided there had been no contact and Boycott stayed, but the West Indies captain, who had been at the slip, persisted in demonstrating his anger for almost two hours.

You could cut the air with a knife and Arthur was obviously just as annoyed as Kanhai. At the close of play he quickly got changed, packed up his things and left the umpires' room. I tried to make it clear that it would be better if he ignored the whole incident, but he did not want to discuss it and went his own way.

Even so, I was amazed next morning to see newspaper headlines which read 'Test Umpire in I'll Quit Threat'. Arthur had clearly reached the end of his tether. He argued that the players did not respect the umpire's judgement any more and that the enjoyment had gone out of the job because there was so much at stake. When I reached Edgbaston before 9.00 am Arthur had made up his mind. He put his gear into his case, shook my hand and said: 'I'm going home. I am not taking any further part in this match.'

He wanted an apology from Kanhai. I understood his point of view – he felt his integrity had been challenged by the prolonged nature of the protest. Only Kanhai, by expressing his faith in Arthur's honesty, could put matters right. A number of officials tried to get Arthur to relent and continue, but he remained adamant.

With the ground filling up some action had to be taken and an SOS went out to Charlie Elliott at Leyton. He was ready to come to Birmingham, but could not make it for the start. Meanwhile the West Indies refused to make an apology and their manager Esmond Kentish joined in the talks aimed at finding a solution satisfactory to all concerned.

I could do the bowlers' ends, but somebody had to be at square leg.

Chairman of selectors Alec Bedser and the Warwickshire secretary Leslie Deakins put their heads together and came up with Alan Oakman, the former Sussex and England batsman, who was coach at Edgbaston. He had been on the umpires' list and although he did not relish the idea, he agreed to help out. I made one last appeal to Arthur, who stayed in our dressing room. 'I respect you as a man and as an umpire and I hope you will come out with me,' I said, but he steadfastly refused.

I went to see Kanhai and England's captain Ray Illingworth, and they both accepted that Alan would stand at square leg. In all the excitement he forgot a set of bails and had to run back to the pavilion, much to the confusion of the spectators, who were, however, aware of much that was going on because of the media coverage.

After only one over Fagg had second thoughts and came out to replace Alan. He did not say a word, but I gather that Esmond Kentish had got near enough to an apology to placate him. I was glad to see him, for he held the seniority and we had a bad morning. The West Indies bowled too many bouncers but not enough overs, so that the game reached a kind of stalemate, which did not worry them as they were in the stronger position.

During a bomb scare spectators flood onto the pitch at Lord's as the stands are cleared during the Test Match between England and the West Indies in 1973.

We simply had to have a word with the captains and the little meeting, the first of its kind as far as I am aware, ensured more action in the afternoon, although the Test petered out into a dull draw. Julien and Tony Greig both received final warnings for running down the line of the stumps, which was another unusual aspect of a dramatic game. At the end, I felt tired but reasonably content about the part I had played. I thought I had done as well as could be expected and John Snow said some nice things in the Press about the way I had umpired.

I redirected my concentration to the County Championship again, but unexpectedly got a telephone call from Lord's instructing me to report to headquarters for the third and final Test. 'Dusty Rhodes is not well and the West Indies have asked for you,' I was told. That turned out to be the first of five occasions on which I have been asked to do extra Tests and I was very flattered. Once again, however, events took an unpredictable turn.

There must have been around 28,000 in Lord's on the Saturday with some people sitting on the grass and just after lunch a telephone message informed the authorities that a bomb had been planted somewhere in the ground. With an IRA bombing campaign worrying the whole of London, the Test match presented an obvious target for either the IRA or some hoaxer with a perverted sense of humour.

The police dare not take any risks. Too many lives were at stake and they

advised that the seats would have to be cleared. Billy Griffith, the MCC secretary, made the necessary announcement at 2.40 in the afternoon and most of the crowd wandered on to the pitch instead of making their way into St John's Wood.

There was a good deal of aimless wandering about, but no panic, and the British sense of humour came to the rescue. I reckoned that the covers, which had been wheeled out to protect the pitch, represented one of the safest places to wait, so I sat on them and chatted to the supporters of both sides. The West Indians were buoyant as England, replying to a massive total of 652 for eight, were in danger of the follow-on. Eventually the England players were taken to a tent in the gardens behind the pavilion, while the tourists left for their hotel.

The police, marvellously organized, searched every inch of the stands in about eighty-five minutes, confirming that there was no danger. Someone had caused chaos for his own pleasure and, in doing so, ruined the day for thousands. The time lost did not matter, for England crumbled to defeat by an innings and 226 runs, a margin against them exceeded only once – in the 1946–7 tour of Australia at Brisbane.

After such a fiery baptism nothing could upset me, and ever since I have looked forward to the top games with a keen sense of anticipation. There is nothing like Test Cricket for me and familiarity will never breed the slightest contempt.

The lessons of cricket continually urge winners to be humble and losers to take heart, for fortunes change and the appearance on the scene of youngsters, particularly if they are fast bowlers, encourages hopes of success for any country. Pacemen are the key to superiority in international terms. Often outstanding quickies have hunted in pairs and the record books faithfully document their deeds.

McDonald and Gregory, Larwood and Allen or Voce, Lindwall and Miller, Trueman and Statham, Statham and Tyson, Hall and Griffith, the names go together as naturally as Laurel and Hardy or Morecambe and Wise. The odd eyebrow might be raised by the presence of Gubby Allen's name in that band, but some very good batsmen held him in high esteem. Hutton, in fact, once told me that he still got twinges in his leg on the spot where Allen had hit him with the ball before the war.

Bowlers of this quality do not come along all that regularly and, for instance, Australia had to wait from the mid-1950s, when Lindwall and Miller lost their decisive cutting edge, until the early 1970s, which brought the arrival of Dennis Lillee and Jeff Thomson, to find another really destructive force.

To back up the main thrust of quick bowling, I would always plump for good all-rounders who give you two bites at the cherry. Players such as Ian Botham, Kapil Dev, Richard Hadlee and Imran Khan can fail totally in one direction and yet end up as match-winners in another. The legendary run-makers are well-established in cricket's folk lore, but it is the bowlers who win matches.

One of the most popular trick questions in a sporting quiz asks which English captain toured Australia and never appeared in a Test match. The answer, of course, is Captain Cook, the explorer from the north-east of England, who discovered Australia and, therefore, featured prominently in creating the circumstances which led to Test cricket.

That came about a century after he first sailed into Botany Bay. Many lovers of the game have visited his old house. This now stands in the park just across from the Melbourne Cricket Ground, having been carefully dismantled and transported across the seas to form an Australian monument to his achievements.

Test cricket has now developed to the point at which England and Australia are just part of a growing family. Despite this, there is something special for Englishmen about a joust with the 'old enemy', the men in those distinctive baggy green caps with whom we Yorkshiremen have so much in common. The rivalry has been intense without destroying the spirit of comradeship that has lasted through successive generations.

Eric Hollies, the Warwickshire leg-spinner who bowled Don Bradman for nought second ball in his last Test and prevented him from finishing with an average of 100, became the butt of the Australian crowd's humour during Freddy Brown's 1950–1 trip 'down under'. No matter how hard he tried on the boundary edge the ball kept just eluding his outstretched hand or desperate boot. Throughout the long, hot afternoon he chased hard and hurled himself about to very little purpose, finishing up limp and perspiring. As he stood panting and red faced, the proverbial wag in the crowd shouted: 'What's matter, Hollies, don't they bury their dead in Birmingham?' 'No, they don't,' replied Eric with feeling. 'They stuff 'em and ship 'em out to become Australians.' Typically, he immediately won a lot of friends, because the Australians love a gutsy character. They even gave Harold Larwood a standing ovation as he returned to the pavilion after hitting ninety-eight in the last Test of the 1932–3 tour. As a bowler Larwood may have handed out a physical hammering to their batsmen and been barracked for that, but the Aussies recognized a bonny fighter.

My first Test involving the Australians came in 1975 at Edgbaston, where Mike Denness lost the England captaincy to Tony Greig as his side went down to defeat by an innings and eighty-five runs. I shall never understand why Denness put in the Australians on that fateful first morning of 10 July, for although the weather was overcast, it has been my experience that the ball behaves pretty predictably on this ground. I cannot remember it swinging much and this time the Australians made the most of their good fortune, opening with a stand of eighty between Rick McCosker and Alan Turner.

As this pair ploughed steadfastly on, I pondered the advice that W. G. Grace offered in his days. He said: 'When I win the toss on a good pitch, I bat. When I win the toss on a doubtful pitch, I think about it a bit and then I bat. When I win the toss on a very bad pitch, I think about it a bit longer and then I bat.' This is the best policy in Tests, and would have been particularly so for Denness, who, having been pounded by the Australian pace men in the previous winter, was hanging on to his position as England's leader by a slender thread.

His decision did not make a lot of sense to my mind, because there was also the threat of rain. John Edrich, who had taken over briefly from Denness in Australia, confided: 'We are going to get caught out on this one.' His forecast proved about as accurate as that by the weather men, for when England replied to Australia's first innings of 359, a storm broke over the ground. They were forced to bat on a pitch that got wet on top while staying firm underneath – a real flyer. The outcome was a procession of bemused batsman as Lillee (seven for sixty) and Max Walker (seven for ninety-five) enjoyed themselves to the full.

Only the gallant Edrich, with thirty-four, gave the first innings any substance at all. This was one of those innings in which a batsman's final score hardly reflects the true value of his contribution. The gritty Surrey left-hander may not have been the most stylish player in the game to watch, but he lacked nothing in determination and application.

Poor Graham Gooch completed a disastrous Test debut, collecting a 'pair' and lasting for only ten deliveries. He had been chosen at twenty-one as the youngest to play for England since Colin Cowdrey in Australia in 1954, because the selectors thought he had it in him to stand up to the fast bowlers.

Gooch has massively justified that faith and become one of the top batsmen in the world, but this was a sorry beginning, and I took the time to go and tell him I thought he had been unlucky – caught down the leg side in the first innings and beaten by an unplayable delivery in the second. In fact, only a fine player would have got a touch to the ball from Thomson that accounted for him second time around. Denis Compton felt much the same. He made a special trip to see Gooch to say: 'Don't worry, this sort of thing happens when you are having a lean spell.'

We got a particularly bad batch of balls for this game and several complaints were made. At one stage we had to make a change, but none of the balls Arthur Fagg and I had with us would do, so we sent to the pavilion for a box from

Opening pair – Graham Gooch after being caught at the wicket by Rodney Marsh
for zero in his first Test Match at Edgbaston in 1975.

which to make our selection. An Indian emerged and came running up to us with a number of balls. 'Are you on the groundstaff here?' I asked while we sought a suitable replacement. 'No, I am an Indian Test umpire,' he replied proudly. I did not recognize him and to the best of my knowledge have never seen him again, so what he was doing I shall never discover.

No suitable alternative was available when the second new ball lost its shape in the Australian innings, so we asked for a new ball to be bowled in the nets. John Whitehouse, the Warwickshire captain, hit it about for eight overs. The Warwickshire officials then rushed it out to us, but both sides preferred to continue with the one in use.

After this set-back, England did much more than appoint a new captain. They also 'unearthed' David Stanley Steele, from Northamptonshire, who was

'Old Grandad' – David Steele squeezes away another run during
his remarkable spell of success for England in 1975.

the ripe old age of thirty-three. A dogged batsman with prematurely greying hair which made him look older than his years, he quickly won the admiration of the nation as he got bravely on to the front foot and defied fast bowlers who had carried all before them. He collected fifty and forty-five in the second Test at Lord's to set the pattern for the rest of the summer.

I did not catch up with the Test series until the last of the four matches at the Oval, where Australia easily got the draw they needed to take the series by one match to nil. Steele continued his incredible run there. His scores had been seventy-three and ninety-two in the third Test at Leeds and he added thirty-nine and sixty-six. During his first innings at the Oval Thomson admitted: 'I don't like bowling at "old granddad". He's hard to get out and everybody's on his side.'

I could see what he meant. Steele really did get a long way forward and showed the bowler the spikes in his left boot as he thrust it down to meet the ball. He could also hook – as he showed every time they dropped short at him –

and sometimes he appeared to play the shot while still on the advance. Because of the World Cup, the Test programme continued into September and this one at the Oval proved to be only the second Test to be staged in that month, the other being on the same ground back in 1880.

Statisticians told me that it was the longest game to be played in this country. It must have appeared so as England, replying to a score of 532, were bowled out for 191 and then spent the rest of the time piling up 538 themselves in their second innings.

A lot of English cricket followers were disappointed at their first sight of 'Thommo the Terrible' and the man who had destroyed England during the winter never hit his most impressive form in this country. Thomson had dominated the 1974–5 series, taking thirty-three wickets at only 17.93 runs each, and when he was injured and missed the final Test, battered and bruised England salvaged some pride by winning in Melbourne by an innings and four runs.

In 1977, England welcomed back Geoff Boycott from his three-year exile by regaining the Ashes by three matches to none and this time Lillee missed out because of his involvement with the Kerry Packer organisation. Thomson finished as Australia's leading wicket-taker, with twenty-three, but he rarely caused a lot of concern. Injury had forced him to have his shoulder pinned the previous Christmas and he jarred his right elbow during the tour, but one of the most important reasons for his comparatively modest returns was the uncertainty as to where his front foot would land and he was frequently 'called' for over-stepping.

I umpired the Australians against Somerset at Bath while they were still warming up for the Test programme and no-balled him fifteen times in seven overs. Thomson had been out of the team and struggled to find some sort of rhythm, needing eleven deliveries to complete his second over. He kept shaking his head sadly as I indicated where his front foot was landing and by the time that Greg Chappell took him off, Thomson's seven overs had cost forty runs without bringing a wicket. He had bowled only three overs against Kent at Canterbury previously on the tour and was thoroughly miserable. Nor did he manage to do much about the difficulty, for he had over one hundred no-balls to his name by the close of the tour.

I noticed that after marking out his run and putting down the disc, he tended to start his approach to the stumps from a variety of places, a habit which did not help.

On the swings and roundabouts of international cricket, England had their moments once the fire began to burn low for Thomson and Lillee, although you could never ignore the latter's professionalism. He suddenly produced one of the finest deliveries of all time in Melbourne in 1980 and he took enormous delight in beating Boycott with it so comprehensively.

It helped Australia to win the third Test by eight wickets after England had gone some way towards apparent safety by scoring 306 in their first innings. Australia replied with 477 and then claimed six wickets for ninety-two in a sensational passage of play. I was on a world tour and received an invitation to watch the game from the Australian Board of Control, who have shown so much kindness towards me. While having a chat in the dressing rooms, I saw the start of the England innings on television. Disaster struck when Boycott padded up and had his offstump knocked back by one that cut back sharply.

Silence greeted his return with seven to his credit. 'Did you see it on television?' he asked. 'I did,' I told him, 'and it was as unplayable as makes no difference. It might have been a bit close to leave, but it nipped back like a fire-cracker.' Boycott just gazed into space, muttering to himself: 'I can't believe it, I can't believe it.'

Lillee, inspired by that success, bowled beautifully and quickly disposed of David Gower and Peter Willey to spearhead the victory drive. When the jubilant Australians came off, he gave me a big wink and shouted: 'Still plenty of life in the old dog yet.' I had to agree.

Even he had to take a back seat in 1981, when Ian Botham filled the starring role in two of the most remarkable Tests. The first at Headingley turned the situation upside-down after Australia, already one up, had been on course for victory by an innings. That flashing computerized scoreboard at Yorkshire's headquarters blazed out the news that gamblers could have 500–1 against England winning and at those odds Lillee and Rod Marsh just had to risk a few pounds. Like all Australians they fancy a bet and ran into trouble later for backing the opposite side, but no one suggested they had given less than one hundred per cent when they duly collected their winnings.

England, under Botham's influence, staged a storybook recovery to win after following on, but Lillee and Marsh would have much preferred the glory of victory to the few pounds they picked up from a wild flutter. I did not see that match, but I was with Don Oslear at Edgbaston to witness the other side of Botham's all-round talents. Once again Mike Brearley's team had to fight hard to retrieve lost ground.

Bowled out for 189, they conceded a first innings lead of sixty-nine, which left them at a distinct disadvantage. England did not fare a lot better at the second attempt, scrambling their way to 219 and once more I regarded the tourists as being long odds on.

To be fair, Bob Willis bowled very tight, but the Australians got into the

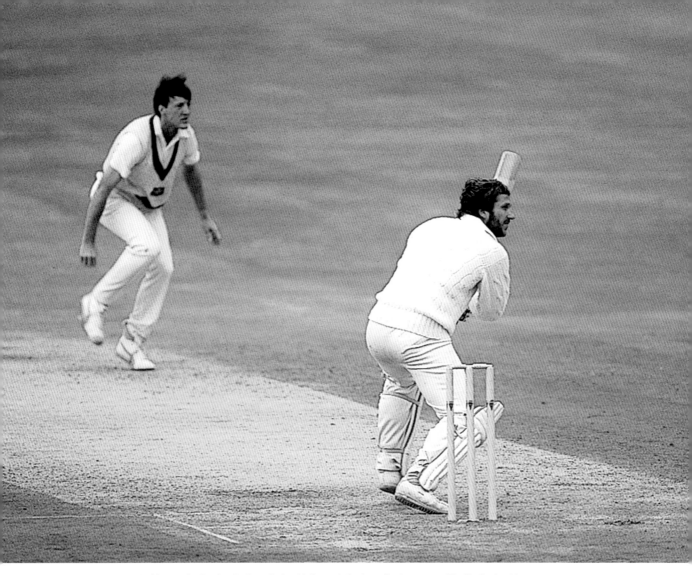

Working a miracle – Ian Botham during his fantastic innings of 149 not out at Headingley in 1981, when England beat Australia after following on.

eighties with only three down and Brearley looked increasingly anxious as he busily tried to revive his team's fortunes. 'What do you think?', he enquired at one stage. 'You've got problems, skipper,' I told him. He obviously had to find someone to link up with Middlesex off-spinner John Emburey, who represented his best hope of turning the tables with the ball spinning a bit.

Botham did not want the job. 'We are struggling,' he told Brearley. 'I don't see how we can get them out on this pitch. It's not swinging for me or bouncing.' Brearley gave me the impression that he intended to call up Willey with his more gentle off-breaks, but he turned back to Botham. 'I've changed my mind,' he announced. 'I want you to have a final fling. Give me all you have got, but for Heaven's sake don't give them anything to hit.'

That was a tall order, but Botham performed a miracle, grabbing five wickets for one run in twenty-eight balls and raising the 10,000 crowd to a fever of excitement. He strutted across the stage like a Shakespearean actor, making the most of the situation and getting himself caught up in the drama.

Botham gets emotionally involved and I can sense when he is 'on song'. His eyes glow with the light of battle and he expects a wicket with every ball. When he is batting, his aim is to hammer everything for four or six. You could almost hear yourself breathing in the silence which marked his approach to the stumps at Edgbaston, but the reaction to each incident brought a deafening roar.

No one could fully grasp what was happening, least of all the Australians, who were stunned. They crashed to defeat by twenty-nine runs – all out for 121 after reaching 105 with only four batsmen out. Twice they had lost Tests they must have reckoned were in the bag and poor Kim Hughes, their captain, confessed: 'I know we can beat England, but we just can't cope with Botham. He's a one-man army.'

That was an accurate enough assessment, but although there would be no argument about the Man of the Series, those two old campaigners Boycott and Lillee refused to leave all the limelight to one individual. Barrie Meyer and I had the best seats for a rare old battle between them in the sixth Test at the Oval, where Australia got the better of a draw.

Brearley got some stick for fielding first after winning the toss because the Australians got 352 – a total based solidly on an opening stand of 120 between Graeme Wood and Martin Kent. It was quite hazy, so there ought to have been some swing, and I gathered as I got ready that England's senior professionals did not exactly see eye to eye over what was the best course of action. It is easy to be wise after the event and I did not join the knockers. England were in no real danger as the strips at the Oval mostly get easier towards the fifth day.

They reached 100 for one at the close on the Friday and Lillee had been some way below his best. Operating down wind he did not manage to match the hostility of Terry Alderman, wasting the new ball by pitching it well wide of the stumps. He got rid of Wayne Larkins, but Boycott and Chris Tavaré were content to let him use up his energies.

What a difference a day made! On the Saturday, Lillee simply shed the years and bowled magnificently. He took seven for eighty-nine, his best Test figures, and kept them all on the hop. His battle royal with Boycott took the eye because it was classic stuff. Neither bowed the knee an inch and the Yorkshireman challenged Lillee in terms of quality by scoring 137.

Lillee proved that the pitch would allow a little bounce. In one spell he struck

*Ian Botham celebrates his 200th Test wicket after Rod Marsh is caught by Mike Gatting,
England v. Australia, The Oval, 1981.*

Boycott on the helmet, the jaw and the shoulder. The batsman peered quizzically down the pitch, but there was not even a hint of intimidation. 'I'll not overdo the short stuff,' promised Lillee and he kept his word. When he finally had Boycott caught superbly by Graham Yallop, Lillee said: 'There's more than one damned good player in this series.'

The facts and figures backed up that claim. Boycott had completed a record sixty-first Test half-century, Brearley held his fiftieth catch and Bob Willis passed Wilfred Rhodes' tally of 109 wickets against Australia. Botham picked up

his 200th Test wicket, Marsh reached the 3,000 run mark and Yallop got to 2,000. Australia did not look for victory in that last Test, being more concerned with not losing again, but probably regretted not being more positive. England, chasing 383, got to 261 for seven, so with more time at their disposal the visitors might have won. Lillee gained yet another success over Boycott – lbw for nought – and had the honour of being named Man of the Match.

Years ago, the visits by the Australians, which occurred roughly every four years, were awaited eagerly, but more recently the West Indies have been every bit as popular with the English public, drawing a huge following from among their own country-men who have settled in England and are bringing up families. They have held the title of unofficial world champions for quite a while and there is no doubt that their much-discussed visit in 1976 stands out as one of the highlights of my career as an umpire.

The weeks before that tour were scarred by controversy following bitter arguments in the Caribbean, where Indian captain Bishen Bedi protested strongly about what he believed to be intimidatory bowling. He declared his side's innings closed at 306 for six in the first innings of the fourth Test in Kingston, Jamaica, with Ansuman Gaekwad, Brijesh Patel and Gundapa Viswanath all hurt. India's second innings finished at ninety-seven with only five wickets having been taken because no other batsman was fit enough to continue the contest.

The importance of keeping an eye on short-pitched bowling from the start could not be overstressed and I had to take action when the West Indians met Sussex at Hove.

Wayne Daniel, a relative newcomer to the side, went absolutely flat out to impress and put a lot of effort into his bowling. He could be very swift, but he did not keep the ball up sufficiently and Arnold Long had to get out of the way of four bouncers in one over. I had to give Daniel an official warning, which was in addition to one I had issued earlier about running down the line of the stumps in his follow-through.

(Facing page)
Geoff Boycott is hit by
a bouncer from
Dennis Lillee, but went
on to score a century in
the 1981 Oval Test
between England and
Australia (above).

This upset Daniel and wicket-keeper Deryck Murray, the acting captain. These events took place in the afternoon and when we came off for tea I met Donald Carr, who informed me that the Test and County Cricket Board had appointed me to stand with Tom Spencer in the first Test later that week. Arthur Fagg had withdrawn with a back strain. Well, I thought to myself, at least I have made it clear where I stand on short-pitched bowling.

When we arrived at Trent Bridge for the Test, I discovered that Daniel had gained promotion to the West Indian team in place of Michael Holding, who had been taken to hospital with suspected glandular fever.

The big lad from Barbados had to wait his turn, for Viv Richards slammed England all over Nottingham to make 232 and I had plenty of time to admire the sheer perfection of his innings. Daniel did very well to take four for fifty-three as England battled away to avoid the follow-on. He admitted that he had taken my remarks to heart at Hove and had tried hard to get things right in the nets in the short time at his disposal.

With his slightly amended approach, he whipped the ball into the right-handers from fairly wide of the crease and proved an even bigger threat to the left-handers, who had to contend with deliveries moving across them and away towards the slips. Brian Close had an especially hard time against him. Closey, England's youngest player in 1949 when eighteen years and 149 days, gained another distinction as the second oldest to represent them since the war, being forty-five years and 100 days on the first day of this Test. Gubby Allen was forty-five years and 245 days when he played against the West Indies at Kingston during the 1947–8 trip, when the bowling was presumably a bit less demanding.

Full of guts, Close got right into line for the first ball from Daniel and edged it to slip, where Gordon Greenidge put the chance down.

We had a busy time one way and another. A swarm of bees flew across the field on the Saturday, stopping play while the players and spectators took what cover they could, and I can confirm that from close range they presented a frightening sight. One journalist, trying to get to the truth of the matter, came up to me at close of play and asked: 'Can you tell me if they were bees or wasps? I want to get it right.' 'I have no idea, mate.' I replied. 'Not one of them stopped buzzing long enough for me to find out.'

Then Chris Old collected a bizarre boundary, edging a no-ball from Daniel into his stumps and wide of the startled wicket-keeper. After this a flock of pigeons decided to use the area behind the bowler's arm as a landing strip and practised aerobatics, disturbing the batsmen so much that we made several unavailing attempts to shoo them away.

Sunil Gavaskar examines his broken leg after Ian Botham hit him with a drive
during his innings of 208, England v. India, The Oval, 1982.

In their second innings the West Indies sent on their twelfth man, Collis King, to act as runner for Greenidge, who had a strain. We would not allow this, of course, and they should have known better.

The laws clearly state: 'The person acting as runner shall be a member of the batting side and shall, if possible, have already batted in that innings.' Larry Gomes came out and did the job instead. We told Old to roll down his sleeves when bowling. A bandage covered the spot on his forearm where he had been hit while batting and it distracted the batsmen.

I share one record with David Constant, for in 1974 at Old Trafford we became the youngest pair of officials to stand in a Test. I was forty and David thirty-two.

The opposition that year came from the Indians, who I have found to be charming and polite whatever the situation, yet for some reason best known to themselves they objected to David taking part in the first Test of the 1982 series. All the first-class umpires gave him a massive vote of confidence and, as far as I can discover, the tourists had come across him only in the Yorkshire fixture at Bradford, where, to the best of my knowledge, there were no doubtful decisions or arguments. David said he could think of nothing that might have shown him in an unfavourable light.

I umpired in the second and third Tests – at Old Trafford and the Oval – both of which finished in draws. Alan Whitehead made his Test debut with me at the Oval, where Ian Botham slammed a furious double century and, in the process, inflicted some painful damage on poor Sunil Gavaskar, the Indian captain.

Fielders crowd in very close to the bat in the hope of picking up catches from the little nicks on to the pad and are obviously in considerable danger when Botham is at the wicket. Boycott can, I think, claim the credit for christening him 'Guy the Gorilla', following one of the Christmas parties on tour when the Somerset man dressed up in an animal skin.

He possesses that sort of strength and this enables him to give the ball a fearful crack. Gavaskar crept in almost to within touching distance to the bowling of left-arm spinner Ravi Shastri, possibly encouraged by the gentle nature of David Gower's dismissal to a little dab stroke which gave the wicket-keeper a simple catch. Hardly had Botham arrived when he made contact against one that pitched short with a square cut that carried all the weight of his powerful arms. The ball struck Gavaskar a sickening blow on the shin and he needed assistance to make his way to the pavilion in obvious agony. India lost their best batsman proving the risk had not been worth taking.

Derek Randall chipped in with a perky ninety-five and he and I had a narrow escape. Dilip Doshi offered Botham a half-volley which came back down the pitch like a thunderbolt. We did our best to take evasive action, but I fancy that neither of us was quick enough. Thankfully the ball whistled inches over our heads on its way to the boundary.

Constant returned to Test duty for the second of the three matches against Pakistan, who achieved a morale-boosting ten-wicket victory at Lord's, where their dashing young opener Mohsin Khan hit 200. He endured the nerve-racking frustration of being on 199 for three hours while we waited for a heavy downpour to relent before he finally nudged his way into the record books with that important extra run.

Another fascinating statistic attached itself to the England innings. They batted badly in reply to Pakistan's 428 for eight declared, being dismissed for 227 and having to follow on.

The biggest contribution to that moderate total came in the shape of forty-six extras, with a world record of thirteen wides.

*Man in the middle. Bird talks tactics during a crowd disturbance in the inaugural Test
between England and Sri Lanka at Lord's in 1984.*

Constant had to put up with an unnecessary show of petulance from Abdul
Qadir which soured the proceedings. It was good to see a leg-spinner featuring
so prominently in a Test attack and bowlers such as Qadir and India's more
recent discovery Laxman Sivaramakrishnan bring a welcome extra dimension
to the game. Nevertheless, Qadir appeals so fiercely that what is basically a
question becomes a demand, and he proved very insistent when Botham,
missing a sweep, was struck on the pad. Constant said it was not out, but Qadir
continued to jump up and down with his hand raised aloft. David came over to
me. 'I think we shall have to stop play if they don't accept the ruling,' he said.
'The best thing to do is have a word with Imran,' I advised, and the Pakistan
captain, Imran Khan, helped us to sort things out.

Frantic appealing spoiled this Test, and former England batsman Tom
Graveney, who graced the scene in the 1950s and 1960s, pointed out that
umpires had become the target for what, in some cases, could be described as
nothing less than intimidation. 'When I came into cricket, a batsman who knew
he had touched the ball usually gave himself out and that was that,' he said,
adding: 'Nowadays, hardly anyone walks.'

Players should realise, however, that we can act only as we see things. Attempts to put on pressure change nothing. They can, though, lead to umpires retiring early. Tom Brooks, a top Australian official, told me that he came close to quitting in the middle of a game because he had become sickened by a refusal to accept his decisions. He soldiered on, but later retired prematurely and his departure took away a fine umpire that cricket could ill afford to lose.

What a difference when the Sri Lankans appeared in their inaugural Test at Lord's in August 1984. A much-respected judge dismissed them as 'not much better than a university team', but they competed brilliantly, led England on the first innings, and remained polite, sporting and charming throughout. They had to put up with two demonstrations, sparked off by trouble at home concerning the minority Tamils. Their openers, Sidath Wettimuny and Amal Silva, barely got to the wicket before we suffered an interruption. On to the field came the publicity seekers. I concentrated on defending the pitch, but the batsmen were really shaken and Wettimuny asked: 'How can we do ourselves justice? I am so worried.'

He had every right to be and another disturbance took place later, but the Sri Lankan players kept their heads to win a host of friends and admirers with their uncomplicated attitude. I wish that more people had been there to see the Sri Lankans, for only 32,428 went through the turnstiles, but those that did got real value for money.

Not all Test cricket is a matter of life or death and there is time for a bit of fun, so long as it never looks like getting out of hand or damaging cricket's image. While England were beating New Zealand at Trent Bridge in 1983 Allan Lamb brought a handful of jumping crackers on to the field and when I reached the bowler's end dropped one or two behind my back which made me jump about.

It is not unknown either for Botham to wait until I have got into the bath and then creep in to pour a bucket of ice cold water over my head.

These pranks enable us all to let off steam because Test cricket definitely makes everyone tense. At Edgbaston in 1981, Australian captain Kim Hughes had to dodge and weave as Bob Willis pounded in and let fly with one or two short deliveries. 'You had better start spacing them out a bit, Bob,' I warned. 'That's all right, Dickie,' Hughes said. 'This is Test cricket not a tea party. I expect things to be tough.'

Around the World

T<small>HE MERE THOUGHT OF TRAVELLING</small> around the world in eighty days proved so appealing that it gave rise to a book and a film. Well, it is possible to cut that time by quite a bit in these days of jet travel and I can claim to have made the trip in four weeks. I covered 46,000 miles in that period on a sponsored tour that took in lectures on umpiring and coaching in cricket techniques.

With an itinerary that reads like a travel agent's brochure, I visited Bombay, Singapore, Hong Kong, Sydney, Melbourne, Auckland, Wellington, Christchurch, Tasmania, Sydney (again), Perth, Sydney (for a third time), Bombay (again) and finally got back to London feeling rather dizzy and wondering just where I was. At one stage I went down with a slight tough of sunstroke in Sydney, where my mind was reeling with all the time changes.

The doctor who called in the hotel to look at me came, by coincidence, from Leeds so we had a good old fashioned chinwag on all manner of topics from the changing face of the city to the state of Yorskshire cricket. With typical bluntness he said, after prescribing some tablets: 'Whoever arranged your itinerary is either a genius or a madman.'

Despite the fatigue that dogged my footsteps towards the end, it was an adventure I would not have missed for anything, for I met some really tremendous people and enjoyed wonderful hospitality.

Snags cropped up here and there just to make life a shade more interesting. When I flew into Bombay from Sydney, I got the VIP treatment. Even at 10.30 in the evening about 10,000 people crowded into the area around the airport pushing and shoving their way hither and thither. A number of officials resplendent in a variety of uniforms took great pains to assure me that I would be well looked after, saying: 'Do not worry Mr Dickie, we will give you priority. You will soon be through passport and customs control.' This comforting message continued to reach me at regular intervals, yet not until 4.30 in the morning did I finally limp through the formalities. I dare not think how long I would have been kept waiting had I not been given special clearance.

Sunil Gavaskar is caught at the wicket by Bob Taylor off Ian Botham during the Jubilee Test between India and England in Bombay, 1980.

The Jubilee game between England and India captured the imagination of the whole nation, who followed events very closely. Cricket is without question the game out there.

I have also been to Calcutta and seen the crowds for Tests at Eden Gardens. It is by no means rare for some 85,000 spectators to squeeze into the stadium, leaving another 85,000 trying to gain admission, and I discovered that, in accordance with long-standing custom, tickets are generally duplicated and sold twice. Thus, when an Indian appeals for lbw, the 85,000 inside the ground support him immediately and the 85,000 outside add their voices seconds later as news of the possible success for the home team reaches them via radios and word of mouth.

England won the Jubilee Test, arranged to mark the fiftieth anniversary of the founding of the Indian Board of Control, and I proudly watched Graham

Stevenson, a lad I saw grow up down the road at Ackworth, make his international debut. 'Stevo' took two wickets and scored twenty-seven not out in that ten-wicket triumph.

A real bonus came in the shape of an eclipse of the sun which meant a day off. Not a solitary figure ventured out on to the streets and I spent the time stretched out on my bed catching up on some sleep. What bliss! When I moved on, Geoff Boycott came up and pushed a bundle of letters into my hand, 'Will you post these for me when you get back to England?' he asked. I put them in my luggage and did not notice until I stood before the post box in London that he had neglected to put any stamps on them.

While in Sydney I managed to see Harold Larwood, who lived near the Oval and who has settled very contentedly in Australia, despite the wrath that descended on his head during the bodyline series. He is a great character, full of common sense about cricket and with strong feelings about what is right and wrong. I spent a fascinating few hours learning about his experiences and what it was like to be a professional in an era usually referred to as 'the good old days'.

He left me in no doubt that the ordinary cricketers' lives were hard, for they had to know their place and enjoyed none of the perks which are part and parcel of the present set-up. One big difference between then and now relates to the fact that before the advent of the John Player League players always has Sundays off. Larwood made a habit of having a night out on the Saturday and liked his pint. He usually met up with his great colleague, Bill Voce.

Harold Larwood, pictured at Trent Bridge during the 1977 Test Series between England and Australia.

Once, having enjoyed a convivial evening, they emerged from the public house in a mellow mood. Voce, discovering a wheelbarrow in the yard, suggested that Larwood should have a ride down the street. Off they set, but had not got very far before the noise attracted the attention of a policeman, who did not take too favourable a view of their antics. 'Let's have your name, then,' he demanded, confronting Voce and taking out his notebook. 'I'm Bill Voce, the Nottinghamshire and England fast bowler,' came the reply. 'Oh yes,' said the policeman sarcastically, 'and I suppose that is Harold Larwood in the barrow?'

Long distance travel, of course, needs plenty of planning and I am lucky to have a sound team at my back. John Williams, the manager of Thomas Cook's in Barnsley, invariably makes sure that I get to the right place at the right time, while my local chemist, Brian Ellison, keeps a whole range of medication available to cover any eventuality. Despite their best endeavours, however, I have had one or two scares in the farther flung corners of the sporting world.

When I visited Dubai with a party from *The Cricketer* magazine, for instance, I really got myself into a terrible muddle. As usual, I had several hours to spare after arriving in London by mid-afternoon for an evening flight. I called into a café for a time-consuming cup of tea and casually checked that I had everything with me that I needed. A sudden surge of panic overtook me when I realized that I did not have my passport and I remembered with sickening certainty leaving it on the desk in my study. Instead of being able to make my way to Heathrow at leisure, I faced an emergency and the hands on my watch began to race round.

A frantic dash across London got me to the offices of British Airways in record time and I breathlessly poured out my story. 'You can't go. There is nothing that can be done,' an official announced, adding, as an after-thought, 'unless you try the passport office.'

Sweat poured off me as I rushed down the street and made my way to the only place where I had any hope of sorting things out. I do not like to use my name to seek favours, but when I saw the people queueing in the passport office I had to do something. I realized all too well that in a few minutes they would be closing down for the day. Pushing my way to the front, I informed a somewhat startled young lady: 'I'm Dickie Bird, the Test match umpire, and I must see the man in charge.'

Thankfully he appeared at once. He happened to be a keen cricket follower, so he recognized me and pulled out all the stops to help. 'If you can get a quick photograph of yourself, we'll process you a passport straight away,' he promised. Off I ran, still carrying all my luggage, which by now weighed a ton. I cannot remember what the pictures looked like, but they must have shown a very dishevelled man as I took them, almost without pausing for breath, in one of those booths on a tube station. Somehow we got through all the details and, clutching the vital document, I completed the journey to Heathrow literally with seconds to spare before I had to book in for my flight.

There is a lot of interest in cricket in the region around Dubai and Sharjah has become a minor centre for the game. My first trip there was just about as hectic as my scramble to collect that passport. I went out to umpire in the Asia Cup in 1984, when India won it to add to their triumph in the World Cup in this country.

The competition took place in March and April and before agreeing to

Umpires Bird and Swarup Krishnan during the 1984 Asia Cup in Sharjah.

officiate I made it clear that I would have to be at the April meeting of the Test and County Cricket Board in London, since attendance there is part of my contract. The Asia Cup organizers readily agreed to pay all my expenses to fly back for the meeting, so I stood in two matches, came home, got off the plane at Heathrow in the morning, went to Lord's, played a full part in the discussions and the following morning climbed back on to a plane for the return journey to Sharjah, where I soon got back into action.

This, though, is not the only time I have covered thousands of miles to satisfy conflicting demands on my services. During the England *v.* Australia Test at Trent Bridge in 1977, Rodney Marsh came into the umpires' room to tell me that there had been a telephone call from Australia for me. Suspecting some outrageous leg pull, I did not react with any enthusiasm. 'It's straight, really,' he insisted, 'and I have taken a number for you to ring them back.' Convinced of his sincerity, I checked on the time difference and at 9.30 that night made contact with Bill Currie, a television advertising executive, who wanted a 'father figure' to appear in some commercials. 'The Australian players have suggested you,' he continued, 'so we'd like you out here as soon as possible.'

In the middle of a Test, I obviously could not just drop everything. 'England needs a few runs yet to beat your lot,' I said, 'but I do have a few free days next week.' I pointed out firmly that I had to be back in time for the Gillette Cup semi-finals, but we were off on the merry-go-round. I flew out to Australia, got to my hotel at 6.00 in the morning. After breakfast the television company picked me up and I spent a full day on the filming. The following day, Dennis Lillee invited me to the studios of Channel 9, Kerry Packer's TV station, and I commentated on live pictures of the Headingley Test from England. After an exhausting two days, I was back in the air heading for home.

The Asia Cup was the brainchild of an Arab businessman with a tremendous passion for cricket. Abdul Rahman Bukhatir controls more than thirty commercial operations and has spent a small fortune on fulfilling a childhood dream. The game has been played around the Arabian Gulf for a number of years, mainly under the influence of the English businessmen and engineers. No doubt a lot of Arabs have been mystified by the sight of the English going about this strange ritual with all the complicated rules, but gradually they are picking up the finer points and Bukhatir told me: 'I think it is wonderful to be able to bring some of the best players in the world to my country. There are so many aspects to cricket. It has a much wider scope than any other sport I have come across.' For this reason, although cricket is not officially recognized by the Supreme Council for Youth and Sport in the United Arab Emirates, Bukhatir pressed on with his imaginative scheme. Neutrality and non-profitability are his watchwords and he has founded a benefit fund which has already paid out over £300,000 to Asian cricketers. His remaining ambition is to see a United Arab Emirates side competing against Test-class opposition and he may not have to wait all that much longer.

Many obstacles had to be overcome and back in 1977 they were handicapped by some very rough grounds. Undeterred Bukhatir laid down a grass pitch and provided, at a staggering cost of £2 million, permanent stands to accommodate the increasing number of spectators. There is now comfortable room for 12,000. One constant threat comes from the sandstorms which can be terrible. I experienced one and saw some of the tents being blown out into the desert, where, for all I know, the cutting winds ripped them to shreds. I brought the players off because we could not see a thing. Former Yorkshire and England all-rounder Dick Hutton took part in that game and as we fled for shelter I could hear him shouting: 'I can't see you Dickie, give us a call so we can find the pavilion.'

Bukhatir, whose boyhood hero was that legendary Pakistan opening batsman Hanif Mohammed, loves mingling with cricketers and has built on the impressive beginnings. John Hobbs, covering the competition for *The Cricketer*, soon realized that he had to be pretty quick to grab a decent seat in the limited Press Box. One day he lost the keys to his wife's car in his haste to secure an adequate vantage point. They were returned by a smiling Arab, who politely handed them over. John explained the situation and the Arab said: 'It was the will of Allah to save your marriage.' I do not think John's wife was too pleased when the keys went missing, but that was taking things a bit too far.

Rothmans stepped in to sponsor the four-nation tournament when England, Australia, Pakistan and India did battle in March, 1985. All the games turned out to be low-scoring affairs, with India and Pakistan setting the pattern. We used some stumps which I took out from England, courtesy of Duncan Fearnley, and by the time I arrived my arms ached. It's a long way from Barnsley to Sharjar with seven stumps to carry, I can tell you, and they don't fold up for convenience.

India managed only 125 in that opening fixture, which received massive coverage in the local press and was attended by the Ruler of Sharjah, His Highness Sheikh Sultan bin Mohammed Al Qasimi. Imran Kahn had a sensational six for fourteen return from his ten overs, but India's new batting star Mohammed Azharuddin also caught the eye and his forty-seven came from a really high-class innings.

Pakistan then collapsed against accurate bowling, with the spinners Laxman Sivaramakrishnan and Ravi Shastri demonstrating that accuracy rather than speed is the principle virtue. They dismissed Pakistan for eighty-seven and set the stage for the eagerly awaited clash between England and Australia. Meanwhile, Tony Lewis approached me on behalf of the BBC and asked me to do an interview for Radio Four. I agreed, but hardly expected what followed. 'We shall have to go out into the desert,' Tony said, setting off to find a taxi.

Having secured a cab we shot off, although the driver appeared to have little idea as to where he was going. On we bumped and shuddered and I began to fear the worst, while Tony remained determinedly cheerful. At last we came across a tin hut, from the roof of which protruded a radio mast. The temperature had soared to around 114 degrees as we sat down and contacted London with the aid of a man who sat on the roof holding wires. By some miracle the conversation got through all right and we received word back that the reception had been excellent.

England and Australia literally stopped the show. The Aussies scrambled home by two wickets with their winning run coming from the last possible delivery. England scored 177, which, by comparison with other efforts, represented a good effort, particularly as some members of the side admitted that the arduous tour of India had left them very tired. When the Australians edged home they were greeted by a fanfare from a variety of horns, while the crowd also let off hundreds of firecrackers. The traffic stopped for fifteen minutes while the result spread around the surrounding area.

Not surprisingly, the final turned into a pretty nervy affair and out in the middle you could sense just how tense the players were, so it was definitely not a case of going through the motions. Both sides wanted to win all right.

India did the trick by three wickets, after restricting Australia to 139 with Shastri again in useful form. They had become a formidable force after their failure against England and I feel they will be a power in the world for quite a while yet. Among the English lads, I think that Robert Bailey, from Northamptonshire, did himself a lot of good. He possesses a keen eye and hits the ball with a nice flowing full swing of the bat, so he is one to watch for the future.

Lagos is another emerging country from the cricket point of view and I spent a week or so there in November and December 1980 doing some coaching. That little expedition got off to a bad start, however, because on the day I had to fly out the tickets had not arrived. Feeling helpless at home in Barnsley, I got in touch with the Nigerian airways, with whom I was flying. They assured me that the tickets would be left at the airport, but I remained uneasy about so loose an arrangement, for I am only too aware of how easy it is for things to go wrong in the hustle and bustle of airports. Since I had a late departure time, I popped into Lord's to check with Donald Carr, who quickly brought his influence to bear and sorted things out. Confusion followed me to Lagos, because when I arrived no one appeared to meet me – except that is a welcoming party of about 30,000 very hungry mosquitoes, who promptly set about having a nice meal – at my expense!

The airport staff casually booted my luggage from one end of the reception area to the other, ignoring my protests, and I really had a sense of fear. I consulted my letter from the West African Cricket Conference, who were responsible for making all the arrangements, and noticed a list of three hotels. My prospects of finding any of them on my own in broad daylight would have been strictly limited. In the dark they were hopeless, so I needed some assistance, and persuaded a security guard at the airport to guide me.

He somehow got a taxi which rumbled down a series of dirt roads unmarked by signposts but liberally covered with pot holes that jarred and shook my weary limbs. The fact that the first two hotels we tried had never heard of me hardly settled my shattered nerves and I hardly dared to ask as we arrived at my last address. What a relief when it proved to be third time lucky. Yes, they were expecting me. Yes, the room was ready and waiting. Slumped down on my bags I could have fallen asleep on the spot.

Unbelievably out of the night came a voice I recognized. 'Birdy, what the heck are you doing out here at this hour when all decent folk are tucked up in their own beds?' David Bell, from Hull, loomed up out of the darkness to shake my hand warmly and remind me that the world really is a small place.

He happened to be working for a firm in Nigeria and knew the ropes well enough to settle me in and raise my spirits. It was not such an out of the way place after all.

Unfortunately, next morning did not bring any further developments. No one telephoned or arrived at the hotel. I lingered over breakfast, worrying about what action I ought to take. An Englishman came up and said that he could see I had problems, so I told him the whole story. 'Well, I'm going back to London, via Paris, this morning. I'll see if I can get you a seat on the same plane if you like,' he suggested. Two other Englishmen joined in the conversation having recognized me, and one of them advized: 'You need a lot of patience out in this country. Don't panic because nothing is done in a hurry.'

They took me to the British consulate who got in touch with the Nigerian cricket authorities. Officials duly appeared, very apologetic and full of excuses, having met the wrong flight and assumed I must be coming later, but once things were cleared up I had a superb time.

There is a spectacular sports complex in Lagos with a football stadium which seats 95,000. I saw the World Cup qualifying tie between Nigeria and Tanzania as the only white man in such a huge gathering.

The West African Cricket Conference provided a car and a driver – a big help in enabling me to fulfil all my engagements. I could not have managed without the chauffeur, for the traffic in Lagos is impossible to describe. The volume is too much for the roads, so drivers are only allowed to use their cars on certain days, according to the registration of the vehicles.

There are plenty of English people in Nigeria and they took care of me in the evenings. One drawback, however, came in the form of an electricians' strike which left the hotel without running water for three days. 'What am I supposed to do for a bath?' I asked the manager. 'Open your fridge,' he said, 'you will find bottled water in there'. Try to imagine having a good scrub down in a couple of pints of water and you will get a good idea of the impossible job I had. It took hours.

Actually, Nigeria boasts some gifted cricketers and I spotted several boys who gave the impression that they had it in them to become quality players with the right sort of coaching and competition. These are essentials if any advance is to be made, but I should not be surprised to see standards improve dramatically in the next few years. The desire to do better is very much in evidence.

When the time came for me to leave, Numa Uzoh, secretary of the Nigerian Cricket Association, handed me a letter for the customs on which he wrote: 'At a cocktail party arranged in his honour by the association, several groups presented Mr Bird with an ebony walking stick, a carving of the head of the Oba of Benin in his regalia and a yellow traditional dress with a cap to match. This letter is aimed at soliciting your co-operation in ensuring that he takes his gifts home.' It did the trick in Nigeria, and I marched through customs without any trouble although they did raise one or two eyebrows at Heathrow.

I have received many presents while on my trips abroad and some of them are quite valuable. Sadly this means that they have to be kept in the bank vaults, for burglars have given me some heartache in the past and it is not worth the risk of keeping things in my own house. That's a pity, for I get little pleasure from the things that should remind me of my adventures.

The Kenyan Cricket Umpires' Association invited me to Kenya in 1983 and I stayed in the Treetops Hotel, where thirty-one years earlier the Queen learned of the death of her father, King George VI. Fire destroyed Treetops, an all-wooden building, in 1955 but it has been completely rebuilt.

The management employ a guard because you have to walk about two hundred yards from the car park to the hotel and the wild animals that roam about are always on the lookout for a tasty morsel. When I stayed there the chap on duty hailed from Lancashire, so we were able to bring up all the old rivalry. Elephants try to demolish the hotel periodically, butting it with their heads and rubbing against it so vigorously that the building shakes. Baboons regularly take tea on the veranda by the simple means of stealing bread and cakes from the visitors, so there is never a dull·moment.

Nearby is the grave of Lord Baden Powell, founder of the worldwide boy scout movement. It faces on to the snows of Mount Kenya and is alongside the tombstones of people killed by elephants and rhinos during the pioneer days. Lord Baden Powell lived in a place called Paxtu from 1938 until his death in 1941.

Probably my most dangerous moment came thousands of miles away in the Caribbean, however. While swimming in the seas off the coast of Barbados during a short visit I came into accidental contact with a Portuguese Man of War and collected a nasty sting. Startled, I lashed out but succeeded only in throwing the thing on to my back.

From there it inflicted further pain and damage. I appreciated that I must get some treatment at once and needed an injection, so I rushed from the sea and up the road towards the nearest area of population. It is a far cry from England and medical assistance is not the easiest thing to find, but I luckily came across an old lady selling clothes. She showed great presence of mind, jumping up with amazing agility to cut a lime from a nearby tree to use on the wounds.

She then got me to the doctor. I could not have hoped to find him on my own, but he treated me and said: 'Tonight you will get the shakes all over your body, but do not worry. Tomorrow you will start to feel better and soon you will be well again.' It is a good job he gave me that warning, because otherwise I would have died of fright. I had a really bad night recovering and I often wonder what would have happened to me if that little old lady had not been so kind and resourceful.

One thing is sure – she did not know me. But I have come to marvel at the number of unusual places in which those of us associated with English cricket are regarded as famous people. The game really is international.

Amsterdam, for instance, is not exactly a noted centre. I went there to talk to the Dutch umpires and was taken to a restaurant called L'Abberge Maitre Perre in the Annex Hotel. All round the walls were pictures of celebrities such as Shirley Bassey, Liz Taylor, Richard Burton and other stars from the entertainment business. No sooner had we sat down than the owner appeared.

'May I say how honoured I am to have Mr Dickie Bird, the great umpire in my restaurant,' he said. 'Surely, I can't be so famous in your country where you play so little cricket,' I said. He threw up his arms. 'Everyone knows you. Please send me your autographed picture and I shall give it a place of honour on the walls,' he insisted. After I promised to forward one, he refused to accept any payment for the meal. 'You must be my guest,' he said, offering a bottle of cool gin as a present. I still have that bottle and incidents such as this please me a lot, not because of any sense of personal glory, but because they reflect the significance of cricket.

Whether we realize it or not, those of us who are readily recognized have a big responsibility for furthering the game and ensuring that its image is good all over the globe.

The White Rose

Calling the odds –
Bird responding firmly
to one of the many
incidents which have
cropped up over his
long umpiring career.

I HAVE ONLY ONE REGRET IN LIFE – leaving Yorkshire to join Leicestershire in 1960, even though I followed a path well-trodden by so many exiles. I wish now that I had remained with my native county, playing in the second team if necessary and waiting for the occasional chances in the senior side. I will always be a Yorkshireman at heart, so there was no real satisfaction in turning out at Grace Road. This is why I am so sad to see what is happening at the club.

It makes me angry to read in the papers and hear on radio and television that Yorkshire have become a laughing stock, for nothing could be further from the truth. They still have more members – more than 10,000 – than any of the other first-class counties and I reckon there is a greater number of teams, both great and small in terms of ability and size, competing regularly throughout the Broad Acres than anywhere else in the world.

In addition to the senior organizations such as the Yorkshire, Bradford, Central Yorkshire and Huddersfield Leagues there are a lot of minor competitions, some of which use public playing fields in the evenings to satisfy their appetite for cricket. All of them provide scope for a fierce rivalry that equals anything on the Test match scene.

The rows which thrust Yorkshire into the unwelcome spotlight of media attention have been caused because all those involved care so much that they refuse to accept any form of compromize. Yorkshire are, however, struggling and one of the reasons has to be the persistent squabbling. How can David Bairstow and his young team operate to the fullest extent of their ability against a bitter and divisive background?

Other factors affect Yorkshire's fortunes, notably the many overseas players who strengthen the other counties, and I am certain things would be different if these world-class Test stars went out of the game. At the same time, it has to be admitted that there is not quite the same pride in playing for the county as existed when I first reached the nets.

Captain courageous. Umpire Tom Spencer watches as Ray Illingworth bowls
during the Test Series between England and New Zealand in 1973.

Then Yorkshire were feared throughout the world. They polished off the weaker opposition as often as not in a couple of days and even the tourists regarded their fixture with them as being the equivalent of an extra Test. When I received an invitation to show them what I could do I felt ten feet tall. The journey to Headingley involved two bus rides and a cold wait for the connection, but that was nothing. I would cheerfully have walked from Barnsley and later played without financial reward.

The lads I came across shared this feeling for cricket and we, the chosen few, were regarded with envy. Getting to the nets represented no more than the first step along a hard road and youngsters were soon made aware of the high standards demanded. The slightest slip brought a stern word and the ultimate threat – banishment back to the leagues.

Mike Parkinson travelled up to the nets as a raw recruit with me and we both endured the sharp edge of Arthur Mitchell's tongue. The county's chief coach stood watching us bat without comment. When we finished, he spoke to Mike, who had wrestled bravely with keen bowling that pierced his nervous defence too often for comfort. 'Where are you from lad?' 'Barnsley, Mr Mitchell.' A thoughtful silence, during which we shuffled our feet anxiously. 'What do you do for a living?' 'I'm a reporter on the *Barnsley Chronicle*.' Another pause while Arthur considered his next words carefully. 'Well, if I were you, I'd stick to newspapers.'

Poor Mike just gazed at the floor and probably wished it would open up and swallow him, but he squared his shoulders and said to me as we sadly wended our way home: 'I'll show him.'

Perhaps Arthur wanted to make us angry enough to pull out all the stops, but he stuck to a simple, straightforward principle. You could either sink or swim, and if you had a weakness he wanted to find out at once before he had wasted any of his valuable time. There were no half measures, very few kind words and only the toughest survived.

The system, however, produced so many talented performers that many had to move on – some to gain England honours. Ray Illingworth captained his country after being released and Brain Close earned a Test recall as a discard, having extended his career with Somerset. Brian Bolus flourished so brilliantly with Nottinghamshire that he collected seven 'caps', while Jack Birkenshaw and Chris Balderstone had similar success with Leicestershire.

Brian Close, another giant of Yorkshire, hits out during his later career as captain of Somerset.

Willie Watson, a left-hander in the classic mould who also gained recognition as a soccer intentional, was another Yorkshireman to give Leicestershire a boost and the Midland county have done well out of these rejects. Watson actually persuaded me to join him at Grace Road. Attracted by the thoughts of regular Championship exposure, I asked Yorkshire for my release twice only to be knocked back, but when I persisted they finally gave in and off I went.

It turned out to be a different world. Leicestershire were really in a poor way. There was neither atmosphere nor tradition. You might as well have been batting in a graveyard. I have heard it suggested that Yorkshire's glorious record of achievement is a millstone around the necks of the youngsters who have fared disappointingly in the 1970s and 1980s. That may be true, but let me assure them that there is nothing worse than operating under a cloud of indifference surrounded by empty seats. Silence bites deep into your determination and affects you more than barracking.

An air of resignation hung over Leicestershire until Mike Turner, their resourceful manner, and Tony Lock, that aggressive Surrey and England left-arm spinner, came along to breathe ambition into the club. Illingworth did a lot to bring them fame, but the credit for the initiative belongs to this dynamic duo.

The Leicestershire committee and their far-sighted chairman Charles Palmer also get a pat on the back from me for allowing Turner to put his plans into practice unhindered by a lot of discussions and interference. Turner has gone on year after year, making a profit for the county in the most difficult circumstances and creating a team who have more than held their own. His record, in fact, raises a significant point, for I think Yorkshire would benefit from having a smaller administration. There are too many voices raised in the running of affairs. When I played we had a huge selection committee. I clearly remember being at the wicket at Bradford in 1959 on 150 not out. I watched the committee get up and leave the balcony to hold their selection meeting. Surely, I reasoned, they cannot leave me out after this, but they did. 'Well played, Birdie, now get a move on – you are going with the second team,' said Brian Sellers as I slumped exhausted in the dressing room with 181 not out to my name.

Frustratingly, I did not know with whom to press my case, for among so big a gathering the question as to who said what and which way individual votes were cast became confused. I must say, though, that I had no axe to grind with Sellers. A blunt man who used strong language, he said everything to your face, good or bad, and nothing behind your back.

He tended to want things his own way, but he ran a tight ship and commanded both loyalty and respect. He created some fear as well. He had a habit of appearing out of nowhere in the nets and dressing down anyone he found with his hands in his pockets.

'If I catch you standing like that again, I'll make sure you never get another chance here,' he snapped at the red-faced offender and the warning inevitably did the trick. He behaved just the same as captain.

In 1947 Arthur Booth, the veteran left-arm spinner who featured briefly after the war, filling the gap left by the tragic death of Hedley Verity, was enjoying a rest on the boundary edge between overs. As a forty-four-year-old doing Yorkshire a favour, he no doubt felt the need to take things easy. Without thinking, he slipped his hands into his pockets and followed events from a comfortable distance, untroubled by the ball coming in his direction.

Towards the end of the over, a voice from the ring of spectators seated nearest to the playing area whispered: 'He's got his eye on you, tha's in bother.' Carefully avoiding his captain's gaze, Arthur realized what the friendly warning meant, so he calmly took out a handkerchief and vigorously blew his nose as he marched towards the stumps to resume the attack. Sellers moved to intercept him. 'It's a good job you had a handkerchief in your pocket, but you won't get away with it twice,' he said.

Whatever he did or said to them in private, Sellers always stuck up for his men in public, as did Ronnie Burnet, the last of Yorkshire's amateur skippers. The return to the professionals has altered the way sides are run, for they are on the same level in many ways as their colleagues and rarely exert the same sort of influence. Yorkshire enjoyed a long-standing reputation for taking a firm line over discipline, with the amateur captains demanding total obedience, and they seldom hesitated to dispense with the services of players they felt had overstepped the mark or 'outlived' their usefulness.

Brian Close's sacking in 1970 made the headlines, but there have been others. Frank Lowson and Bob Appleyard were shocked not to be re-engaged at the end of the 1958 season, while the dismissal in the same summer of Johnny Wardle, who had a disagreement with Burnet, created a sensation. Wardle took six wickets for forty-six against Somerset at Sheffield at the end of July, but during this match the county announced they were not retaining him, despite the fact that he had been chosen to go to Australia with the MCC in the following winter.

The left-arm spinner was picked for the next game – the Roses clash with Lancashire at Old Trafford, but then left out when it became clear he intended to put his case in the columns of a newspaper. I was called up from the second team and reported to Middlesborough with a tall, gangling left-arm slow bowler called Don Wilson. He played while I did the fetching and carrying as twelfth man and marked his debut by taking five for thirty to help bring about victory over Essex.

The remarkable thing about the Wardle issue was that in its shadow Yorkshire found the spirit to overcome the loss of so fine a bowler to win the Championship in the next year – 1959. Wardle possessed one of the shrewdest aspects of cricketing brains and fully understood the subtle aspects of the game. Like Illingworth, he put his mind to everything and I learned a lot from him.

I believe we had a harder life in general in the 1950s and 1960s and travelling presented many difficulties with the playing hours having to be shaped to fit in with the railway timetables. However hard the authorities tried, snags cropped up, and Jack Birkenshaw and I once had to make a desperate trip.

Yorkshire Colts were playing Cheshire at Hull in June 1959 when the call came from Headingley informing the two of us that we had to go straight down to Bournemouth to join the first team for the Championship fixture against Hampshire. We had to chase 221 to win in the second innings at Hull and Ted Lester, now the Yorkshire scorer and then the Colts' captain, sent Jack and myself in first. 'You had better get on with things and then set out for Bournemouth,' he said. Jack soon gave a catch hitting out, but I did not want to throw away my wicket, so I retired hurt for thirteen.

Even so, we were cutting it very fine and had to run from the ground, still in our whites, our cricket boots sending sparks from the pavement as we galloped along with our clothes under our arms. Panting we scrambled aboard the London train. The railway line runs back past the ground and we were able to look out of the window and wave to our team-mates who were busily chasing those runs.

The contest ended with Yorkshire on 211 for eight, but with me on the train, that was really nine and Freddy Millett, the Cheshire captain, pulls my leg about the incident, claiming that I almost gave his side victory.

David Bairstow, formerly of Yorkshire and England, in action behind the stumps.

The story does not have a happy ending, for Yorkshire lost by twenty-eight runs at Bournemouth, although I had the consolation of top scoring with sixty-eight in the second innings.

How marvellous it would be if Yorkshire could recapture some of the magic from days gone by and rise up like that 1959 squad to restore the county's pride. That is a big task, but back in 1958 spirits were low and even the committee publicly acknowledged that the season had been about the worst in their history.

David Bairstow has plenty of talent at his back, but they need help to deliver the goods. David is still stretching his wings as captain, although I am certain he has it in him to be a commanding leader. He is such an enthusiast that, given luck at the right time, he could be a formidable driving force. To create the right circumstances, Yorkshire would be better with a committee of about ten working under a strong chairman with everyone pulling in the same direction.

I appreciate that this would mean altering the time-honoured system of district representation, but this has been subject to amendment before and the Yorkshire cricketing public are all realists. They understand the importance of streamlining the administration. Those to whom I have spoken – and quite a few come up for a chat – agree that some consideration must be given to change.

The merging of, for example, Halifax and Huddersfield seems logical and, to ensure a proper chain of communication, complaints, requests or suggestions could be channelled through the secretary's office. A small, tightly-knit group could then concentrate on running the club's affairs to the best advantage.

One of the saddest aspects of all the in-fighting has been the loss of Norman Yardley, Michael Crawford and Billy Sutcliffe. They slipped into the background when the committee lost a vote of confidence and their wide-ranging expertise must be missed, however keen and well-meaning the new administrators.

Similarly, it is not easy to see how Yorkshire would have been better off had Geoff Boycott been sacked. Obviously he has been at the centre of the dispute, but his form never suffered and his steady flow of runs gave the team a solid, reliable base. He is not the easiest man in the world to know and he shuts himself away, but his awe-inspiring contribution to Yorkshire cricket has to be recognized.

I remember Geoff very clearly as a youngster coming to the Barnsley nets and I batted alongside him to the bowling of a tremendous character called Alf Broadhead, who did a lot for both of us in helping to solve problems with our respective techniques. I have to admit that the signs of greatness in him escaped me. He looked a good county cricketer in the making, but no more than that. Usually, whenever we meet I make this point, and I have said to him many times: 'You've done a lot better than I thought you would. Did you think back in those days at Barnsley that you would become such a prolific scorer?' I never

Hitting out – Geoff Boycott during his century for England against Australia at Trent Bridge in 1977.

get an answer. Geoff just smiles to himself, so I don't suppose I will ever find out just how much he expected when he began his career.

Don Brennan, the former Yorkshire and England wicket-keeper, who sat on the committee as one of the representatives from Bradford, first proposed that Boycott be replaced as captain in 1977, yet I regard him as one of the best leaders on the circuit. He seldom misses a trick and is so wrapped up in his chosen profession that he devotes all his energies to studying the game. He might have become an outstanding England captain had he been more fortunate or had Yorkshire been more successful in the 1970s.

Boycott has attracted more attention than anyone else in first-class cricket. When he was eventually replaced as captain by John Hampshire for the 1979 season a wave of support for him grew. The volume of this public opposition to official policy contrasted sharply with the quiet acceptance of things at Old Trafford, where David Lloyd had to make way for Frank Hayes.

David, by the way, told me that when he and Boycott were the respective captains in the Roses matches the only time they fell into conversation was when they tossed up, and then the exchanges covered no more than the calling of heads or tails.

Perhaps because he is such a controversial and well-known figure, Boycott does guard his privacy as far as he can. Even when invited to his home at Woolley, I had to climb over the automatic gates to gain admission. After pressing the button which enabled me to speak to the house, I discovered that the gates were stuck and could not be opened. Up and over I went, swinging from the branch of a convenient tree like Tarzan. We then sat and had toasted cheese sandwiches, watching the workmen lay out out his tennis courts as we talked about cricket. When I finally left, he called down the drive after me: 'Don't damage the lawn as you go out.'

Another interesting little exchange I had with Boycott came during a Sunday League fixture at Huddersfield in 1980. On a good batting pitch, he picked up runs quite easily before experiencing some trouble with his contact lenses. 'Just hold this for me a minute, Dickie,' he said, putting one of them in the palm of my hand. Unfortunately, a strong wind immediately blew it away. Frantically he looked around, but as far as I could tell it must have been yards from us. 'Those cost a lot of money,' he said, looking slightly annoyed.

He fished about in his pocket and produced another. 'Don't lose this,' he instructed, but I had no chance. Before I could close my hand, it followed the first one away into the outfield. 'We'll have to find it, I haven't any more,' Boycott insisted, and there we all were on our hands and knees seeking the proverbial needle in the haystack. We had no hope, and at last he had to retire when Bob Willis demanded that we get on with the game, as time was running out and he did not want to lose any overs.

Yorkshire's run of poor performances has raised doubts about the quality of the youngsters coming through, but there are still some exciting prospects, including, of course, Martyn Moxon, the opener who has quickly made it up the ladder to England status. He, like me, hails from the Barnsley area, which has been a prolific breeding ground. Boycott, Graham, Stevenson, Arnie Sidebottom and Ian Swallow also hail from Barnsley and have progressed through the coaching system run by the Wombwell Cricket Lovers' Society.

This organisation is world famous and its strength underlines the deep-rooted love of the game in Yorkshire. It was formed in 1951, when a small group gathered to listen to Wardle. About twenty attended that first meeting and now the membership is around 600. Jack Sokell, the Yorkshire committee man, has been the only secretary and Leslie Taylor the only president.

One of Wombwell's main activities is coaching and I have spent many happy hours helping out in this direction. The lads who go on to county cricket are a real bonus, but there are hundreds, I guess, in the leagues who had some connection with the Society. There is a tremendous satisfaction in coaching, because you can see a boy steadily improve. I try whenever possible to make practice sessions like the real thing, telling those taking part to imagine that they are in a game in which every run and every wicket is vital.

Increasingly I am asked why Wombwell should have the most famous of all cricket societies. It is after all little more than a dot on the map and sometimes not even that. It has, nevertheless, a proud place in the history of cricket as the birthplace of Roy Kilner, that very great Yorkshire all-rounder who died at the height of his powers when thirty-seven in 1928. He had been on a coaching visit to India with Maurice Leyland during the winter and was attacked by para-typhoid fever. Although rushed to Barnsley Fever Hospital, he did not recover, and it was estimated that 150,000 people attended his funeral – or at least were in the town for that purpose.

In a sense his memory is preserved, for Leslie Taylor married his sister, Molly. His spirit is very much in the Wombwell Society and I am sure he would have approved of schemes to send boys to Scarborough College for a week on a cricket scholarship.

Moxon, whose father Derek, also did a lot of coaching until he, too, died at a tragically early age, owes something to Wombwell and still takes a keen interest in the society, having worked his way to the fringe of what I bet will be a long England career.

I have noticed as well the potential of such as Paul Booth and Steven Rhodes. Booth, a left-arm spinner, comes from another area with a jealously guarded tradition for producing exceptional talent – Huddersfield. He will not be rushed. That is not the way of things in Yorkshire, so he is not likely to hit the headlines for a year or two, but he has superb control and flights the ball so well. When the basics are right the good coach can polish a boy's game without too much effort. The correct ways come naturally and it is as much a matter of quiet guidance as anything. Paul possesses a good temperament, which is so vital, so I intend to study his progress carefully.

High hopes are held about Rhodes, although sadly this outstanding young wicket-keeper left Yorkshire to join Worcestershire. Having made great strides in the Bradford League and at junior representative level, he decided to move on when he found his path persistently blocked by David Bairstow.

He was in an impossible situation. He realized he must get experience in the first-class game, but wicket-keepers are like goalkeepers – you can have only one in a team and it really is a teaser for a county when they have to pick between two who are both up to county standard. Yorkshire wanted to hang on to Steven but could not guarantee him a place in the senior side.

Tim Boon, now with Leicestershire, took a similar view. He missed part of the 1985 season after breaking a leg in a car crash in South Africa, but he is on my short-list of players with a big future. He has taken a season or so to come through, but he strikes the ball hard and times his strokes well.

Outside Yorkshire, I recommend cricket followers to take note of Neil Fairbrother, from Lancashire. He is left-handed which makes him particularly valuable since teams like to have a touch of variety in the top half of the order. This complicates life for the bowlers, who have to switch their lines of attack constantly, while the field has to be adjusted frequently. Lancashire, of course, have a lot of left-handers, but this is likely to even itself out and Fairbrother has a neat compact style and moves his feet well.

I also believe the best of Graeme Fowler is yet to come. I keep reading that the perky Lancashire left-hander is out of his class in the England team and he will have to be replaced. This is possibly because he is ready to take on the bowlers around the offstump. When he gets out the critics jump to point to a weakness. I rate him highly, though. Fowler is a very gutsy competitor with a consistent record and a high percentage of good scores. He coped doggedly with the pace of the West Indians and punished the Indian attack as England restored their pride during the winter tour of 1984–5. For my money Fowler is quite capable of holding his own with the best.

I sang the praises of Nottinghamshire's Tim Robinson long before he suddenly emerged on England's tour of India in 1984–5 and he, alongside Moxon, has glittering prospects. Fairbrother will not be all that far behind this talented pair.

Whatever else, I look to Yorkshire for signs of general encouragement. It is said that a strong Yorkshire means a strong England. The same theory is advanced in Australia about New South Wales and in the West Indies about Barbados.

Peter May, when he became chairman of the England selectors, repeated this sentiment. I am sure it is true now more than ever, with Yorkshire being the only county to rely on home-grown players, so the county's fight is not a parochial affair.

I read the remarks of new cricket chairman Tony Vann at Yorskshire's pre-season luncheon in 1985. 'Yorkshire, relying on people born inside the county, have something that none of our opponents possess – local pride,' he said. That is very much the case. It cannot be just coincidence that Geoff Boycott, Chris Old and myself, all Yorkshiremen, turned down the Packer approach for the same reason. We cared too much about our roots.

The Future

CHAPTER

13

Bird with Larry Gomes,
England v. West Indies,
Edgbaston, 1984.

As long as I can remember – and according to the game's historians, since the earliest days – first-class cricket has had to contend with financial problems. Many counties have scraped along on the breadline, having, as we say in Yorkshire, to make do and mend. That they are still in existence is a tribute to the hard work and vision of so many people who have overcome all manner of handicaps to achieve minor miracles of survival.

It is because of this background that I firmly believe the future is bright. There will, of course, be difficulties, but cricket's grass roots are firmly established and the game is spreading at the highest level.

The emergence of Sri Lanka is clear proof of that and, after travelling the world to coach and lecture, I can vouch from first-hand experience that there are many pockets of enthusiastic and quite skilful players all eager to gain greater experience.

Obviously things have changed a lot in the past twenty years, the biggest development being the extension of the limited-overs competition.

As a result, we have had floodlit cricket and coloured clothing, which has certainly not pleased the traditionalists. I do not imagine that either will become part of the English scene because our climate is not suitable, but the use of the white ball is another matter.

John Hampshire, the former Yorkshire, Derbyshire and England batsman, is among the county players who have expressed some interest in experiments in this direction.

John, now an umpire, has argued for some years that the red ball is easily lost against the background of the spectators' highly coloured clothing. Two or three years ago, after a match at Scarborough, he told me: 'Dickie I could easily have been killed. I was fielding on the boundary and just never picked up the ball which bounced and whistled past my head.'

I honestly do not know whether a white ball and a black sightscreen would make things better, but the idea could be tried out. At the same time, I think the

authorities could consider doing away with leg-byes. These really add nothing to the game and often punish good bowling. I have seen many instances of the ball beating the bat before running off the pads for runs.

This is frustrating enough in Championship fixtures, but it can be crucial in the one-day games, where the leg-bye can add up twenty or even thirty to the score. Umpires have to rule out the runs if they feel the batsman has not made a legitimate attempt to play the ball, but that is never an easy decision to make. Some players push forward with the bat close to, but slightly behind, the pad and get away with the leg-byes. I have heard it suggested that legislation to do away with leg-byes would encourage bowlers to attack the leg stump, but, on balance, I think the benefits outweigh the disadvantages.

Even so, the matter ought to be studied carefully, for with the best of intentions it is still possible to get things wrong. Take the lbw law, for example. Fifty years ago the 'new law' was introduced, largely as a consequence of the bodyline series of 1932–3. This meant that batsmen could be given out to balls pitched outside the off stump and the vast majority of cricket legislators thought this a very good thing. Most have subsequently changed their minds, however, so the need to tread carefully is obvious. All I claim is that consideration should be given to these theories.

The future depends also on cricket's ability to sell itself to the public and, here too, the signs are hopeful. Many county clubs have launched well-organized campaigns to attract spectators and members, although the profits from Test matches remain the major source of income. One of the game's great appeals is to the family, particularly on the smaller, friendly grounds. Happily, mum, dad and the children can still go along, watch the experts and then have a go themselves during the intervals. This is unique to cricket. You can't go on and have a kick-about at half-time in a soccer match, nor can you enjoy a few rallies at any time during the Wimbledon fortnight.

I love to see places such as Scarborough, Chesterfield or Cheltenham crowded with spectators all enjoying their own little contests on the boundary edge. The kids get involved in the game and, whether they are any good or not, are likely to become enthusiasts in later years.

Of course, they have to use soft balls because leather balls would be dangerous in the circumstances, but that is by no means a bad thing. Youngsters can play without the fear of being hurt and learn quickly.

I am less happy about the bad behaviour of the minority of spectators who spoil the enjoyment of others. I had a frightening experience at Chesterfield during Derbyshire's Benson and Hedges Cup tie with Gloucestershire on the day of the 1985 FA Cup Final. Our match was progressing quietly, with

Tearful farewell – Bird takes the field at Lord's for his last Test Match, England v. India, 1996.

Gloucestershire batting, when the peace and quiet of that beautiful ground was shattered by a gang of hooligans.

Presumably celebrating the victory for Manchester United over Everton at Wembley, they came, draped in red-and-white from the town end straight across the field, stopping play as they danced and chanted slogans. Paul Romaines, the Gloucestershire opener, looked at me and said: 'What are we going to do about this? We can't tackle all that lot.' Since there were about thirty invaders I agreed with him, and there wasn't a policeman in sight. I suppose that is, in one way, a tribute to the average cricket-watcher, but it was a small comfort to us as we stood back and hoped nothing too serious would happen. Thankfully, the drunks – there is no doubt that drink influenced their antics – finally disappeared, but they had underlined how vulnerable we are to the law-breakers and the thoughtless.

Even such people as these, however, will never destroy the game and I expect to be keeping an eye on the progress of all the counties long after I have hung up my white coat. There might be more than seventeen teams by then, for expansion could be just around the corner. There is a substantial following for cricket in the north-east and the Durham area could well support a first-class club. We might also introduce a system of promotion and relegation, and my old friend Ray Illingworth has put forward one very attractive scheme of this sort.

Playing staffs may have to be trimmed, however. The days when boys were ready to hang about and wait for their chance have gone. Better educational opportunities and a wider range of jobs – despite unemployment – mean that sometimes sport comes a long way down a youngster's list of priorities. Yorkshire coach, Doug Padgett, explained some of the difficulties to me, saying 'When I see a promising junior I wonder as much as anything whether he is going to go on to University, for if he does we will lose him for two or three years and who knows what will happen then.'

Still, the coaching net is thrown wider throughout the country and the best will continue to prosper, keeping cricket, our great national game, in the news for the best of reasons.

Picture Credits

Endpapers © Patrick Eagar; Half-title © Sporting Pictures (UK) Ltd; Title Page © Patrick Eagar; Page 9 © Patrick Eagar; Page 11 © Patrick Eagar; Page 14 © Patrick Eagar; Page 19 © Patrick Eagar; Page 23 © Patrick Eagar; Page 26 © Patrick Eagar; Page 29 © Patrick Eagar; Page 31 © Sporting Pictures (UK) Ltd; Page 32 © Sporting Pictures (UK) Ltd; Page 35 © Patrick Eagar; Page 41 © Patrick Eagar; Page 43 © Hulton Getty; Page 45 © Patrick Eagar; Page 46 © Patrick Eagar; Page 49 © Patrick Eagar; Page 50 © Patrick Eagar; Page 52 © Patrick Eagar; Page 54 © Patrick Eagar; Page 57 © Patrick Eagar; Page 58 © Patrick Eagar; Page 61 © Patrick Eagar; Page 62 © Patrick Eagar; Page 67 © Patrick Eagar; Page 71 © Patrick Eagar; Page 75 © Patrick Eagar; Page 76 © Adrian Murrell/Allsport; Page 79 © Patrick Eagar; Page 83 © Patrick Eagar; Page 85 © Edward Wing/Camera Press, London; Page 87 © Patrick Eagar; Page 91 © Patrick Eagar; Page 93 © Adrian Murrell/Allsport; Page 97 © Patrick Eagar; Page 98 © Patrick Eagar; Page 100 © Patrick Eagar; Page 105 © Patrick Eagar; Page 107 © Patrick Eagar; Page 110 © Patrick Eagar ; Page 113 © Patrick Eagar; Page 117 © Hulton Getty; Page 118 © Hulton Getty; Page 121 © Adrian Murrell/Allsport; Page 123 © Patrick Eagar; Page 124 © Patrick Eagar; Page 125 © Patrick Eagar; Page 127 © Patrick Eagar; Page 129 © Patrick Eagar; Page 132 © Patrick Eagar; Page 133 © Patrick Eagar; Page 135 © Patrick Eagar; Page 143 © Sporting Pictures (UK) Ltd; Page 144 © Patrick Eagar; Page 145 © Hulton Getty; Page 148 © Hulton Getty; Page 149 © Patrick Eagar; Page 155 © Patrick Eagar; Page 157 © Patrick Eagar; Page 159 © Patrick Eagar.